4th Edition

How to
Administer an
Estate

A Step - By - Step Guide for Families and Friends

By
Stephen G. Christianson, Esq.

CAREER
PRESS
Franklin Lakes, NJ

How to Administer an Estate, 4th Edition

Cover design by Barry Littman

Printed in the U.S.A. by Book-mart Press

Edited by Robert M. Brink

Typeset by Eileen M. Munson

To order this title, please call toll-free 1-800-CAREER-1 (NJ and Canada: 201-848-0310) to order using VISA or MasterCard, or for further information on books from Career Press.

CAREER
PRESS

The Career Press, Inc., 3 Tice Road, PO Box 687
Franklin Lakes, NJ 07417
www.careerpress.com

Library of Congress Cataloging-in-Publication Data

Christianson, Stephen G.
    How to administer an estate : a step-by-step- guide for families and friends / by Stephen G. Christianson. — 4th ed.
        p. cm.
    Includes index.
    ISBN 1-56414-523-9 (paper)
        1. Executors and administrators—United States—Popular works. Probate law and practice—United States—Popular works. I. Title.

KF778.Z9 C48 2001
346.7305'2—dc21

00-049850

This book is dedicated ————

to the

William & Mary

"Grad Thing"

My thanks ———————

to Bob Elwell and Rich Gibbons, whose comments and opinions at the Fishmarket Conference Center inspired much of what is in this book.

CONTENTS

INTRODUCTION

According to the United States Bureau of the Census, nearly three hundred million people live in the United States. This statistic means that sooner or later, three hundred million people need to make wills providing for the transfer of their worldly possessions to their spouses, children, and other persons. For each will, an executor must be appointed in order to carry out the person's final wishes in compliance with state laws. Usually people ask someone without previous experience, such as a spouse, relative, or friend, to be their executor. This means that a person close to you may ask you to be his or her executor.

Even if someone dies without a will ("intestate"), the estate still must be administered. Again, normally a surviving spouse or child petitions the court for permission to be the executor rather than see the task performed by strangers or court appointees. Therefore, even if no one asks you to be his or her executor, you could still find yourself taking on the responsibility of administering a loved one's estate.

How to Administer an Estate is a step-by-step guide for everyone faced with the responsibility of becoming an executor of an estate. I have written it to walk you through each of the procedures involved from start to finish, beginning with whether or not you should agree to become an executor.

Chapter 1 discusses whether or not you should agree to become an executor. I have listed several "red flag" or danger signals that indicate potential problems that you might wish to avoid and have a professional handle. I also discuss what intestacy is, and how it affects whether you should agree to be an executor. Chapter 1 ends with an appendix summarizing what each state requires for you to become an executor in that state. This appendix includes each state's residency requirements, and what your potential legal liabilities are as an executor.

If you've agreed to be an executor, Chapter 2 guides you through the difficult period after the person's death. It takes you through legal and personal matters, such as: securing his or her will (if there is one), meeting with the family, taking care of funeral arrangements, dealing with the deceased's employer, banks, attorneys, CPAs, and so forth. Furthermore, Chapter 2 discusses the principle *of joint property,* meaning property that is jointly owned and can go directly to any surviving spouse. The appendix following Chapter 2 summarizes every state's laws on joint property, including technicalities such as intestate-share laws, spousal right-of-election laws, and automatic-share laws.

Chapter 3 introduces you to the first step in the legal system's formal requirements, namely *opening the estate* or filing the first documents with the local courthouse. There is *regular-estate administration* and *small-estate administration.* In addition, Chapter 3 tells you how to get the required court papers, called *Letters Testamentary* if the deceased had a will, and *Letters of Administration* if the deceased didn't have a will. The chapter's appendix summarizes state laws relevant to the estate-opening process, such as issuing formal estate notices to creditors and interested parties and whether there are simplified small-estate procedures of which you can take advantage.

Next, Chapter 4 discusses the first important legal event you will face after you have opened the estate: listing, or *inventorying,* the estate's assets and their value on forms that must be submitted to the court by a deadline. This chapter also takes you through other important details, such as: opening the estate account, collecting the deceased's cash assets and other property, getting the required appraisals of certain types of property, and so forth. The chapter concludes with an appendix that summarizes every state's estate inventory and appraisal requirements.

After the estate inventory, the next steps are the estate taxes and paying off any claims against the estate. I take you through this step-by-step in Chapter 5, which, with the appendix, summarizes all of the state *priority-claim* statutes, when claims have to be presented, and applicable federal and state estate-tax (and other tax) requirements. If the estate has assets that can't be sold off easily, Chapter 6 tells you how to manage the estate. For example, if the deceased had a business or other property that takes time to be sold or passed on, this chapter tells you what to do. The appendix following Chapter 6 summarizes your powers as the executor over the estate.

Finally, Chapter 7 covers the final legal matters. It discusses the required court fiscal accounting of the estate's assets after claims and taxes are paid off, distributing what's left of the estate to the beneficiaries and other people who get property from the estate, and various technical formalities that are required to wind up the estate. There is also a Glossary of Terms at the end of the book.

Although there are state variations on the procedures involved, the principles described in these seven chapters stem from common roots in the old common law of England and thus will be similar in every state except Louisiana and in Puerto Rico. These exceptions are due to the fact that Louisiana law has its origin in the laws of France and Puerto Rican law in the laws of Spain. Although Louisiana law is not so different that I had to exclude it from the fifty-state summaries that follow every chapter, Puerto Rico's system is so different from the principles discussed in this book, that out of prudence, I do not attempt to address it.

Finally, I have two words of advice: don't panic. The maze of different state laws and different forms and procedures may seem confusing at first, but it isn't as bad as it looks. In fact, most people find that being an executor is pretty easy once things get underway. You'll find yourself going to the same courthouse, talking to the same court officials, and your executor duties will become a predictable, simple routine. In fact, with a minimum of legal hassle, you'll be able to achieve the primary goal of being an executor: Helping people adjust to the death of a loved one.

BECOMING AN EXECUTOR

What is an executor?

An *executor* is someone who is legally responsible for administering a dead person's estate. Although the precise legal term is usually *personal representative* or *administrator,* for the sake of convenience, I use the word *executor* throughout this book. Court clerks and other officials will know what you mean.

This chapter concerns what you should do if someone asks you to be the executor of their estate. Usually this question comes up when people are making their wills and want to name their executors in the wills. Of course, you might involuntarily be faced with the question of becoming an executor, such as if a parent or spouse dies without a will. In that case, this chapter will give you an idea as to whether you can handle the responsibilities on your own, or perhaps should seek professional help.

I have organized this chapter in terms of the *Issues* you must look at. First and foremost, you must read the deceased's will. Ask for a copy of the will, or the final draft if it hasn't been signed and notarized yet. Most wills are pretty straightforward. As a guide, I have included a sample form of a last will and testament at the end of this chapter. The critical sections of the will concerning the executor's rights and duties are highlighted. If the will of the person whose estate you would be administering imposes unusual or complicated duties on the executor, think twice before accepting. If you do not feel confident about being able to handle the duties, perhaps someone with more financial or legal experience should take the job.

Executors administer only estates

As discussed more thoroughly in Chapter 2, some types of property aren't part of a dead person's estate, such as jointly-owned property—for example, a house owned by a husband and wife. If the husband dies first, the house automatically becomes the wife's sole property. The reverse is also true: if the wife dies first, the house automatically becomes the husband's sole property. Either way, the house will never be part of either the husband or wife's estate because it went to another person automatically. The executor would not be responsible for the house as part of the estate.

> *Example:* George B. dies. He had a house worth $200,000 and a checking account with $20,000 in it, both jointly in his name and his wife's name, Barbara B. His only other asset was a $10 bill found in his pocket when he died. Assuming that under the laws of George and Barbara's state, Barbara gets joint property automatically, how much of an estate will George's executor have to administer?

> *Answer:* $10. Since the house and checking account are not part of George's estate, all the executor has to deal with is the $10 bill.

Issue 1: How large is the estate?

If the person making the will (the *testator*) is married and has done a good job of estate planning, there should be very little in the estate other than personal possessions such as jewelry, clothing, and appliances. Obviously, this means doing a little digging into the joint-ownership status of property covered in the next chapter. The testator or the deceased might be single or have business interests, however. Therefore, see how much the estate is worth. If it is worth over $600,000, then you may be responsible for seeing that federal and state estate taxes are paid. These tax obligations are not necessarily a big problem, as discussed in Chapter 5, but they definitely mean that you will be spending more time on the estate.

Like Issue 1, the following issues do not necessarily mean that you have to refuse to be an executor. They should, however, make you consider whether your time commitment will be substantially increased, and whether or not your potential legal liability will increase.

Issue 2: Are there real estate or business interests?

Not only might the deceased or the testator have owned his or her house in one name only, but what if he or she owned investment properties? What if he or she owned a business? A merchant might own a store, or a doctor might own a medical practice. Investments, real estate, and/or business interests mean more responsibilities for you as the executor, because profits, losses, and expenses have to be carefully accounted for to the courts and to the heirs of the estate (see chapter 6 for more details). Further, if any real estate or business interests are located in another state, then you will probably have to get an *ancillary administrator* in the other state(s). There may also be additional estate tax and inheritance tax questions. This means more work for you. For example, if the deceased happened to own a winter residence in Florida, you will have to call the courthouse for the Florida county where that property is located and ask how you go about complying with Florida statute 734. 102, concerning the ancillary administration of nonresident property in Florida.

Issue 3: What is the deceased's marital and divorce history?

There are many ways under the law in which former wives or husbands can claim that they are entitled to some or all of the estate. This can happen whether or not there is a will.

> *Example:* You agree to be the executor of your uncle Donald's estate. His will was made in 1989, and states "my wife is to inherit my entire estate." In 1990, Donald divorced his first wife, Ivana. In 1991, Donald married Marla. Donald died in 1992 and never made a new will. Who gets Donald's estate, Ivana or Marla?

> *Answer:* Who knows? Both Ivana and Marla can argue in court that they are the "wife" referred to in Donald's will. There are different legal interpretations among the states as to what such vague language in a will means.

The point is, you don't want to be caught in the midst of a legal battle that could last for years: ask a professional about former spouses and divorces. Further, understand that children can also assert legal claims to an estate: ask about illegitimate children, children by previous marriages, adopted children, or any children that were, or are, to be left out of the will. Lawsuits by the deceased's children can also tie you up in court.

Issue 4: How much estate planning has been done?

This is not a book on estate planning, but as a general principle, people should try to leave as little as possible in their estates. In addition to the forms of joint-property ownership discussed in the next chapter, there are ways of passing property to beneficiaries outside of an estate, through means such as life-insurance policies and trusts. Before agreeing to be an executor, ask how much estate planning has been done. Ask the person if he or she has seen an attorney, accountant, or other professional with skills in estate planning. This is particularly important if there are complicated real estate, business, or trust interests involved. The more estate planning that has been done, the smaller the estate will be, and thus less work for the executor.

You should also encourage the executor to put his or her will in a safe place. Have him or her check with the courthouse to see if the will can be recorded. Once recorded, a will becomes a matter of public record and cannot be lost or destroyed. If you can't record a will in your state, have the testator keep it in a safe-deposit box, or even in a fireproof metal lockbox for the home or office.

Many people leave their wills with their attorney, but I'm against this unless you've known and trusted your attorney for a very long time. Lawyers change jobs, retire, or die like everyone else. Law firms can break up or merge, and the file containing your testator's will might get lost in the shuffle. I also discourage executors from holding the will for the deceased. What if the will is accidentally destroyed in a fire or other accident, and you get sued in a dispute over the terms of the will?

Issue 5: Will you have to administer any business interests?

Despite the best estate planning, some types of property may end up in the estate anyway. For example, doctors have practices and businessmen have businesses. The practice or business could be *sole proprietorship,* which means it is owned and operated by the doctor or businessman alone. It could be a *partnership,* in which ownership and operation of the business or practice is shared by several businessmen or several doctors. There could be other forms of ownership, such as a limited partnership where real estate is involved, or a corporation. Several forms of ownership may be involved.

If a partnership or limited partnership is involved, ask for a copy of the partnership or limited-partnership agreement. The agreement should state what happens if a partner or limited partner dies. It may be that the partnership or limited partnership has to buy out his or her interest. If this is the case, then you won't have to worry about administering any business interest. As the executor, however, you are responsible for seeing that the estate gets a fair price in any such *buyout.* If the proprietorship or limited partnership won't (or can't) pay a fair price, you may have to hire a lawyer to sue on the estate's behalf. You might also have to hire an accountant to determine what a fair price is. Your responsibilities as executor will greatly increase if there is a buyout dispute, and there may be limits on how much of the lawyers' and accountants' fees can be paid for out of the estate.

If a corporation is involved, things get even more complicated. Whether you will have to run the business depends on whether the deceased owned all, most, or only some of the stock. If the deceased owned all of the stock, you will probably have to run the business until it can be *liquidated* (sold piece by piece or as a whole for cash), and the proceeds distributed to the heirs. If the deceased owned less than 100 percent of the stock, then there are other stockholders involved, and they have rights. Ask for a copy of the articles of incorporation and any shareholders' agreement. These documents should state what happens if a shareholder dies. Again, there could be provisions for a buyout, thus the possibility of a buyout dispute. If the deceased owned a small amount of the stock in a big company, such as IBM, there's not much of a problem because you can probably dispose of the stock easily, by simply selling it on the stock market.

I have saved the most common type of business headache for executors until last—the sole proprietorship. You will have to run the deceased businessman's, doctor's, or other person's business until it can be liquidated, or, if specified in the will, passed on to an heir. Note that the law usually presumes that the business must be liquidated, no matter how profitable, unless the will specifically states that it is to be passed on intact to an heir. See Chapter 6 for more information on managing an estate with a surviving business. At this point, however, it is enough that you understand that being the executor of an estate containing an ongoing business means significant responsibilities.

Do you qualify to be an executor?

After reading through the five issues discussed above, you should have reached a decision as to whether or not you're willing to take on the job. If you are, you now have to see whether the law will allow you to be an executor. As discussed in Chapter 3, at some point you will have to *open the estate,* which means getting an official document certifying your status as executor. Many states have restrictions on who may serve as executors. For example, some states won't let a convicted felon become an executor. This chapter's appendix summarizes every state's requirements. Sometimes the courts have a very broad power to deny anyone that the judge or the clerk's office considers "unsuitable." This means that when you open the estate, the court could deny you if there is something unfavorable in your background, like a history of treatment for mental illness, even if the law doesn't specifically state that this is grounds for denial.

The appendix also summarizes each state's rules concerning your legal liability as an executor. Most states say that you are only liable if you commit "gross negligence" or "willful misconduct." Often, this principle is loosely described as the "prudent-man standard," which holds you to a duty to act reasonably, cautiously, and thoroughly in administering the estate. Check with the local courthouse clerk's office for more details.

Last Will and Testament
Of

_____

[The critical sections concerning the executor's rights and duties are highlighted.]

I, _____ a resident of _____ , State of _____ , do hereby make, publish and declare this as my Last Will and Testament, hereby revoking any and all wills and codicils at any time heretofore made by me.

FIRST

I am currently married to _____ .
I have _____ daughter(s), _____ , and _____ son(s),_____ , who are minors and who reside in _____ .

SECOND

I direct that the expenses of my funeral and the expenses of any last illness be paid out of my estate, in such amount as my Personal Representative may deem proper with due regard to applicable local law.

THIRD

I direct my Personal Representative to pay all of my legal obligations and debts (exclusive of any debt or debts secured by a deed of trust or mortgage on real estate, not due at the time of my death or becoming due during the period of administration of my estate). In determining my obligations and debts, I direct my Personal Representative to avail himself or herself of every legal defense that would have been available to me.

FOURTH

I direct that (a) all estate, inheritance, succession and other death taxes and, duties occasioned by my death, whether incurred with respect to property passing by this Will or otherwise, and (b) all the costs of packing, shipping; insurance and other charges incident to the distribution of any tangible personal property herein; shall be paid by my Personal Representative out of the principal of my residuary estate.

FIFTH

I hereby confirm my intention that the beneficial interest in all my property, real or personal, tangible or intangible (including joint checking, savings, certificates of deposit, or money market accounts in any bank, savings and loan association, or credit union) which is registered or held at the time of my death, jointly in the names of myself and any other person (excluding any tenancy in common), shall pass by right of survivorship or operation of law and outside the terms of this Will to such other person, if he or she survives me. To the extent that my intention may be defeated by any rule of law, I give, devise and bequeath all such jointly-held property to such other person or persons who shall survive me.

SIXTH

I hereby give, devise and bequeath all of my property and estate, of whatever kind and wherever situated and to which I may be in any manner entitled at the time of my death, including any property as to which I may have the power of disposition or appointment (my "residuary estate"), to my wife/husband, _____ _____ if he or she survives me. If _____ does not survive me, then I give, devise and bequeath my residuary estate to those of my children in equal shares who survive me.

SEVENTH

My Personal Representative shall have full discretionary power, without order or approval of any court, to take any action desirable for the administration of my estate, including the power to sell at public or private sale, any real or personal property belonging to my estate at whatever prices and upon whatever terms he or she shall deem advisable, to retain, invest or reinvest in any property without responsibility for diversification and without being restricted by any rule of law or court limiting investments, to hold any securities in the name of a nominee, to compromise any claims to the same extent I could, if living, and to distribute in kind or in money, or partly in each, even if shares be composed differently, and to exercise all powers permitted under law.

EIGHTH

(A) Every election, determination or other exercise by my Personal Representative of any right, power, privilege, or discretion granted to my Personal Representative expressly or by implication in this my Will or by law, whether made upon a question actually raised or implied in the acts or proceedings of my Personal Representative shall, so far as permitted by law, be conclusive and binding upon all persons affected thereby.

(B) No person dealing with my Personal Representative shall be required to see to the application of any property paid or delivered by my Personal Representative or to inquire into the expediency or propriety of any transaction or to the authority of my Personal Representative to enter into or consummate the same upon such terms as my Personal Representative may deem advisable.

NINTH

(A) I nominate and appoint _____of _____ State of _____, to be Personal Representative of this Will. Should he or she be unable or unwilling to serve, or fail to qualify within reasonable time after receiving notice of his or her nomination; I nominate _____of _____ State of _____, to be the Successor Personal Representative.

(B) If for any reason it is necessary at any time for the property administration of my estate that there be a Personal Representative who is a resident of a particular jurisdiction in which property forming a part of my estate is situated (whether within or without the United States, and if at such time there is no Personal Representative hereof who is a resident of such jurisdiction, then I authorize my Personal Representative to appoint a special or ancillary Co-Personal Representative who is an individual resident of for a bank. trust company or similar corporate institution qualified to act in) such other jurisdiction, with unlimited power in my Personal Representative to remove, and to appoint substitutes and successors for, such special arid ancillary. Co-Personal Representative when the need therefore arises. Said special or ancillary Co-Personal Representative so appointed shall have the power to act only with respect to those matters which necessitated his, her or its appointment, and shall have no authority to participate in any decision by my Personal Representative as to property not located in the jurisdiction of his, her, or its residence, or as to distribution of income or principal.

C) Except for willful default or gross negligence, my Personal Representative shall not be liable for any act, omission, loss, damage or expense arising from the performance of his or her duties under this Will including the act, omission, loss, damage, or expense caused by any agent appointed by my Personal Representative.

TENTH

If any one or more of my children shall be minors at the time of my death, I nominate and appoint _____of _____, State of _____, to be the Guardian of the person of my minor child or children. In the event that at any time and for any reason _____ fails to become or ceases to be Guardian hereunder, I nominate and appoint _____ of _____, State of _____, to be the Successor Guardian of the person of my minor child or children.

IN WITNESS WHEREOF I have subscribed and sealed and declare this instrument as and for my Last Will and Testament in the presence of the witnesses attesting the same at my request, this _____ day of _____, in the year two thousand and _____, (200___).

_____
(Name)

The above instrument, consisting of _____typewritten pages, including the page on which we, the undersigned, have subscribed our names as witnesses, was at the date thereof subscribed, sealed, published and declared by _____ _____, the aforesaid Testator, as and for his or her Last Will and Testament, in the presence of us and each of us, who at his or her request, in his or her presence and in the presence of each other, have hereunto subscribed our names as witnesses thereto (the final clause of the Will having been read aloud to us by the aforesaid Testator immediately after he or she signed the Will, and this clause having been thereupon read aloud in his or her and our presence and hearing), this _____ day of _____, in the year two thousand and _____, (200 ___).

_____   Residing at   _____
_____   _____
_____   Residing at   _____
_____   _____
_____   Residing at   _____
_____   _____

Before me, the undersigned notary public, on this day, personally appeared _____, the aforesaid Testator, and the three witnesses, known to me to be the Testator and the witnesses, respectively, whose names are signed to the foregoing instrument and, all of those persons being by me first duly sworn, the Testator declared to me and the witnesses in my presence that said instrument is Testator's Last Will and Testament and that Testator had willingly signed and executed it in the presence of said witnesses as Testator's free and voluntary acts for the purposes therein expressed; that said witnesses stated before me that the foregoing Will was executed and acknowledged by the Testator as Testator's Last Will and Testament in the presence of said witnesses who, in Testator's presence and at Testator's request, and in the presence of each other, did subscribe their names thereto as attesting witnesses on the day of the date of said Will, and the Testator, at the time of the execution of said Will, was over the age of 18 years and of sound and disposing mind and memory.

Subscribed, sworn, and acknowledged before me by the Testator and the Witnesses, this _____ day of _____ , 200 .

_____
Notary Public

My commission expires: _____

APPENDIX ONE

Fifty-state summary of executors' qualification requirements (including residency requirements) and statutory liabilities. Includes the District of Columbia and the Virgin Islands. State laws change periodically, so be certain to confirm the information set forth below concerning your state with an authoritative source, such as the court clerk's office, or an attorney if necessary.

QUALIFICATION REQUIREMENTS	STATUTORY LIABILITIES
ALABAMA	
Anyone over 19 not convicted of an "infamous crime" or otherwise unfit can be an executor.	Executor is liable for assets lost due to negligence and for failing to give proper notice to creditors.
ALASKA	
Anyone over 21 not considered unsuitable by the court can be an executor.	Executor is subject to prudent-man standard in dealing with estate assets and is personally liable for estate acts and obligations only if personally at fault.
ARIZONA	
Anyone over 21 not considered unsuitable by the court can be an executor.	Executor is not liable for estate contracts unless executor fails to reveal that he or she is acting on behalf of the estate. Executor is personally liable for estate acts and obligations only if personally at fault.

QUALIFICATION REQUIREMENTS	STATUTORY LIABILITIES

ARKANSAS

Any adult who is not a convicted felon or considered unsuitable by the court can be an executor, but nonresidents must get an Arkansas agent for service of process.

Executor is subject to prudent-man standard in dealing with estate assets and is personally liable for estate acts and obligations only if personally at fault.

CALIFORNIA

Anyone over 18 not considered unsuitable by the court can be an executor.

Executor is liable for any damage caused by his or her neglect or misconduct with respect to any sale of estate assets. Executor is not liable for any damage to estate assets unless as the result of personal fault.

COLORADO

Anyone over 21 not considered unsuitable by the court can be an executor.

Executor is personally liable for estate acts and obligations only if personally at fault. Executor can be held liable for estate contracts only if the executor did not reveal that he or she was acting on the estate's behalf.

CONNECTICUT

Anyone over 18 not considered unsuitable by the court can be an executor.

Connecticut has a procedure by which the executor can obtain virtually complete immunity for all acts in connection with selling property and paying debts of the estate. Executor must obtain the prior approval of the probate court.

DELAWARE

Anyone over 18 who is not mentally incapacitated or convicted of a crime can be an executor.

Delaware law imposes a stringent duty on executor to collect everything due to the estate, to pay the deceased's debts, and to distribute everything that the beneficiaries are entitled to under the will.

DISTRICT OF COLUMBIA

Almost anyone over 18 can be an executor, unless convicted of a felony.

Executor subject to prudent-man standard in dealing with estate assets.

QUALIFICATION REQUIREMENTS	STATUTORY LIABILITIES

FLORIDA

Any resident of Florida over 18 who has not been convicted of a felony or considered unsuitable by the court can be an executor. There are exceptions to the residency requirement for spouses and relatives.

Executor is subject to prudent-man standard in dealing with estate assets and is personally liable for estate acts and obligations only if personally at fault.

GEORGIA

Anyone over 18 not considered unsuitable by the court can be an executor.

Executor can be held personally liable for wrong application of estate assets.

HAWAII

Anyone over 18 and a resident of Hawaii can be an executor.

Executor is personally liable for contracts he or she has entered into on the estate's behalf unless the contract expressly relieves the executor of personal liability. Executor is also personally liable for estate acts during the term of administration.

IDAHO

Anyone over 18 not considered unsuitable by the court can be an executor.

Executor is subject to prudent-man standard in dealing with estate assets and is personally liable for estate acts and obligations only if personally at fault.

ILLINOIS

Anyone over 18 not disabled or convicted of a felony can be an executor. Only residents of Illinois, however, can be administrators (executors of estates where the deceased had no will).

Executor is liable to anyone wronged by mismanagement of the estate.

INDIANA

Anyone over 18 and not incapacitated, convicted of a felony or considered unsuitable by the court can be an executor.

Executor is subject to prudent-man standard in dealing with estate assets and is personally liable for estate acts and obligations only if personally at fault.

Qualification Requirements	Statutory Liabilities

Iowa

Anyone over 18 who is not mentally ill or challenged, physically challenged, an alcoholic, a spendthrift, or considered unsuitable by the court can be an executor.

In small estates, executor is personally liable for payment of the estate's debts to the extent that the assets of the estate would have been subject to payment of debts during normal estate administration.

Kansas

Anyone over 18 and a resident of Kansas can be an executor. A nonresident may be an executor if specifically named in will.

If executor embezzles or converts to his or her own use any of the deceased's property, executor is liable for double the value of the property wrongfully taken.

Kentucky

Anyone over 18 and a resident of Kentucky can be an executor. Persons under 18 can be executors if specifically designated in the will. Nonresident spouses and relatives can be executors if they have a Kentucky resident within the county of probate designated as agent for service of process.

Executor is personally liable for estate acts and obligations only if personally at fault or if he or she failed to disclose in any contract that he or she was acting on behalf of a specifically identified estate.

Louisiana

Anyone over 18 who has not been convicted of a felony and who does not have "bad moral character" can be an executor. A nonresident can be an executor if a Louisiana resident is appointed agent for service of process.

If executor does not act as a prudent administrator at all times, he or she is personally liable for all damages resulting from his failure to do so.

Maine

Anyone over 18 not considered unsuitable by the court can be an executor.

Executor is subject to prudent-man standard in dealing with estate assets and is personally liable for estate acts and obligations only if personally at fault.

QUALIFICATION REQUIREMENTS	STATUTORY LIABILITIES
## MARYLAND	
Anyone over 18 and not mentally incompetent or convicted of a serious crime can be an executor. A nonresident can be an executor if he or she designates an agent for service of process.	Executor is liable for estate contracts only if he or she agrees to be liable, and is liable for estate acts only if personally at fault.
## MASSACHUSETTS	
Anyone over 18 of "proper capacity" can be an executor. A nonresident can be an executor if he or she designates a resident agent for service of process.	Executor is personally liable for estate contracts only if he or she failed to disclose that he or she was acting on estate's behalf. Executor is personally liable for estate acts only if personally at fault.
## MICHIGAN	
Almost anyone over 18 can be an executor. Nonresidents can be executors, but residents are preferred.	Executor is liable for losses arising out of his or her embezzlement, commingling of funds, negligent handling of estate, willful and wanton mishandling, and for any other misfeasance or other breach of fiduciary duty.
## MINNESOTA	
Anyone over 18 not considered unsuitable by the court can be an executor.	Executor is subject to prudent-man standard in dealing with estate assets and is personally liable for estate acts and obligations only if personally at fault.
## MISSISSIPPI	
Anyone over 18 of sound mind and not convicted of a felony can be an executor. Nonresidents can be executors, although residents are preferred.	Executor is subject to prudent-man standard in dealing with estate assets and is personally liable for estate acts and obligations only if personally at fault.
## MISSOURI	
Anyone over 18 of sound mind, not convicted of a felony, and not an alcoholic can be an executor.	Executor is subject to prudent-man standard in dealing with estate assets and is personally liable for estate acts and obligations only if personally at fault.

QUALIFICATION REQUIREMENTS	STATUTORY LIABILITIES

MONTANA

Anyone over 21 not considered unsuitable by the court can be an executor.	Executor can be charged with the appraised value of the estate's inventory, except for debts that were not collected without the executor's fault or losses on just sales of estate property.

NEBRASKA

Anyone over 21 not considered unsuitable by the court can be an executor.	Executor is subject to prudent-man standard in dealing with estate assets and is personally liable for estate acts and obligations only if personally at fault.

NEVADA

Anyone over 18 who is a resident of Nevada and who has not been convicted of a felony or decreed incompetent can be an executor.	Executor is liable for debts to estate that are uncollected due to his or her fault and can be charged with losses incurred by the estate that are his or her fault.

NEW HAMPSHIRE

Anyone over 18 not considered unsuitable by the court can be an executor. Nonresidents can be executors, but the courts prefer residents.	Executor is personally liable for maladministration of estate and waste of assets.

NEW JERSEY

Anyone over 18 not considered unsuitable by the court can be an executor.	Executor subject to prudent-investment law in dealing with estate assets and is liable for waste or misapplication of estate, liable for estate contracts if he or she fails to identify the estate that he or she is acting on behalf of, and liable for, estate acts only if personally at fault.

NEW MEXICO

Anyone over 18 not considered unsuitable by the court can be an executor.	Executor is liable for estate contracts if he or she fails to reveal that he or she is acting on behalf of the estate. Executor is personally liable for estate acts only if personally at fault.

QUALIFICATION REQUIREMENTS	STATUTORY LIABILITIES

NEW YORK

Anyone over 18 and not incompetent, a convicted felon, or not considered unsuitable by the court can be an executor.

If executor commingles estate funds, he or she may be charged with a misdemeanor. Executor is subject to prudent-man standard in dealing with estate assets and is personally liable for estate acts and obligations only if personally at fault.

NORTH CAROLINA

Anyone over 18 not decreed incompetent, convicted of a felony, or considered unsuitable by the court can be an executor. A nonresident can be an executor but must designate a resident agent for service of process.

Executor is personally liable for his or her own wrongful acts and for losses to the estate resulting from failure to exercise diligence and good faith.

NORTH DAKOTA

Anyone over 18 not considered unsuitable by the court can be an executor.

Executor is subject to prudent-man standard in dealing with estate assets and personally liable for estate acts and obligations only if personally at fault.

OHIO

Anyone over 18 not considered unsuitable by the court can be an executor although only residents of Ohio may be executors if the deceased died intestate.

Executor is liable for uncollected debts and losses to estate if personally at fault. Executor must pay double if he or she fails to sell property when required by law or if he or she disposes of estate property for his or her personal benefit.

OKLAHOMA

Anyone over 18 who has not been convicted of an "infamous crime" or decreed incompetent can be an executor. A nonresident can be an executor if he or she designates an agent for service of process who lives in the county where the estate is to be administered.

Executor is liable for debts to estate that are uncollected due to his or her fault and for losses to the estate resulting from "unjust" sales of estate property. Executor is liable for twice the amount of any losses to the estate resulting from "fraudulent" sales of estate property.

QUALIFICATION REQUIREMENTS	STATUTORY LIABILITIES

OREGON

Anyone over 18 who has not been decreed incompetent, convicted of a felony, disbarred from the practice of law, or who is not considered unsuitable by the court can be an executor.	Executor is liable for any act that constitutes a breach of fiduciary duty.

PENNSYLVANIA

Anyone over 18 not considered unsuitable by the court can be an executor. A nonresident can be an executor at the discretion of the court.	If executor breaches his duty toward the assets of the estate, the court may hold him or her liable for interest on the assets.

RHODE ISLAND

Anyone over 18 not considered unsuitable by the court can be an executor. A nonresident can be an executor if he or she designates a resident agent for service of process.	Executor is subject to prudent-man standard in dealing with estate assets and is personally liable for estate acts and obligations only if personally at fault.

SOUTH CAROLINA

Anyone over 18 not considered unsuitable by the court can be an executor.	Executor is subject to prudent-man standard in dealing with estate assets and is personally liable for estate acts and obligations only if personally at fault.

SOUTH DAKOTA

Anyone over 18 who has not been convicted of an "infamous crime" or decreed incompetent can be an executor. A nonresident can be an executor if he or she designates a resident agent for service of process.	Executor is subject to prudent-man standard in dealing with estate assets and is personally liable for estate acts and obligations only if personally at fault.

TENNESSEE

Anyone over 18 not considered unsuitable by the court can be an executor. A nonresident may be an executor if he or she designates a resident to serve as ancillary executor.	Executor is subject to prudent-man standard in dealing with estate assets and is personally liable for estate acts and obligations only if personally at fault.

QUALIFICATION REQUIREMENTS	STATUTORY LIABILITIES

TEXAS

Anyone over 18 who has not been decreed an incompetent, convicted of a felony, or considered unsuitable by the court can be an executor. A nonresident may be an executor if he or she designates a resident agent for service of process.

Executor is liable for losses to the estate resulting from his or her willful neglect in not diligently collecting all claims, debts, and property that the estate is entitled to.

UTAH

Anyone over 21 not considered unsuitable by the court can be an executor.

Executor is subject to prudent-man standard in dealing with estate assets and is personally liable for estate acts and obligations only if personally at fault.

VERMONT

Anyone over 18 not considered unsuitable by the court can be an executor. A nonresident can be an executor, but if the executor is not the spouse, child, or parent of the deceased, the court has the power to approve or disapprove of a nonresident executor at its discretion.

Executor is liable for failing to make proper accounts and for his or her negligence or willfully wrong acts.

VIRGIN ISLANDS

Anyone over 18 of sound mind and not convicted of a felony can be an executor. A nonresident can be an executor, but only if he or she was specifically named as such in the will, and if he or she designates a resident agent for service of process.

Executor is responsible for losses to the estate and uncollected debts due to the estate if personally at fault.

VIRGINIA

Anyone over 18 not considered unsuitable by the court can be an executor. Nonresidents may be executors, but usually have to be related to the deceased.

Executor is personally liable if he or she is negligent or fails to properly defend the estate or estate assets.

QUALIFICATION REQUIREMENTS	STATUTORY LIABILITIES

WASHINGTON

Anyone over 18 of sound mind and who has not been convicted of a felony or a misdemeanor involving "moral turpitude" can be an executor. A nonresident may be an executor, but must designate a resident agent for service of process.

Executor is personally liable if he or she fails to pay creditors when ordered to do so by the court, if due to his or her fault the estate suffers losses, or if debts due to the estate are not collected.

WEST VIRGINIA

Anyone over 18 not considered unsuitable by the court can be an executor. A nonresident may be an executor, but only if appointed as such in the deceased's will.

Executor is liable for his or her negligence or improper conduct.

WISCONSIN

Anyone over 18 of sound mind and not considered unsuitable by the court can be an executor. A nonresident may be an executor, but only if he or she designates a resident agent for service of process.

Executor is subject to prudent-man standard in dealing with estate assets and is personally liable for estate acts and obligations only if personally at fault.

WYOMING

Anyone over 18 not decreed incompetent can be an executor. A nonresident can be an executor if he or she designates a resident agent for service of process.

Executor is subject to prudent-man standard in dealing with estate assets and is personally liable for estate acts and obligations only if personally at fault.

FOR ALL STATES

Except in unusual circumstances, the court will not allow you to be an executor if you have a serious conflict-of-interest situation, such as a potentially large creditor claim against the estate. Further, close relatives of the deceased will have priority if they assert a desire to be executor. For example, spouses usually have priority over children, children usually have priority over distant relatives, and distant relatives usually have priority over persons not related to the deceased.

PRELIMINARY STEPS UPON DEATH

When someone dies and you've agreed to be his or her executor, your job begins. Your legal powers are limited until you formally open the estate, but you can take the following important steps:

Step 1: Find out if there is a will.

If there's a will, get it and read it. Remember what I said in Chapter 1 about keeping wills in a safe place. Even if you saw the will when it was originally executed, you still need to obtain it so you can make copies for the heirs and eventually for the court. If there is no will, then the deceased is said to have died "intestate."

Step 2: Make Funeral Arrangements.

If the spouse or someone else has not already taken care of them, you must make funeral arrangements. Contact the hospital, funeral home, or other place where the body is located and ask when you will receive the death certificate. The death certificate is extremely important: you must submit a copy to the court when you open the estate; creditors and other parties may demand to see proof of death. Finally, a word of advice about expensive funerals: Although funeral expenses can come out of the estate, sometimes there is a limit, and if the estate has many creditors, the relatives might end up paying for any expenses over the state limit (see Chapter 5).

Step 3: Inform all interested parties.

You'll see in Chapter 3 that there are formal legal-notice requirements once the estate is opened. At this point, if you haven't done so already, you should inform any family members who don't know about the death. For now, a phone call or a letter will do. Further, you should contact the deceased's employer, attorney, accountant, business partners, and any other person who had an important role in the deceased's financial or legal affairs. Ask all of these people, including relatives, about the deceased's personal papers, records, and books. These people may be able to provide you with important documents, and also with things such as keys to safe deposit boxes that may contain more documents. You will be responsible for obtaining all such documents, which may include bonds or stock certificates that will now go to someone else.

Step 4: Determine the property of the estate and who holds important interests.

You will need to determine (1) the property of the estate, and (2) who are the important parties that can lay claim to it. You need to get a handle on the various potential competing interests in the estate and who can hold you accountable once the estate is opened. Therefore, this chapter has an extensive appendix, which is divided into four topics:

1. Forms of Joint-Property Ownership. As discussed in Chapter 1, some types of property may pass automatically from the deceased to other people without going through the estate. Depending on the state, these types of property may include one or both of the following.

Tenancy by the Entirety. This type of joint-property ownership can exist *only* between married people. If a husband and wife own real estate, such as their house, in tenancy by the entirety, then when one spouse dies the other owns the whole house. This is called "right of survivorship." As you will see in the appendix, sometimes the deed has to refer specifically to a tenancy by the entirety and/or the right of survivorship. In some states, personal property such as shares of stock or bank accounts can be owned in tenancy by the entirety in addition to real estate. Again, sometimes the document of ownership, such as the stock certificate or the bank agreement for a checking account, might have to refer specifically to a tenancy by the entirety and/or the right of survivorship.

You may be wondering what happens if there's a divorce. The answer depends in large part on the state's divorce laws, which are outside the scope of this book. Usually, however, after a divorce tenancy-by-the-entirety property (whether real estate or personal property) becomes either (1) joint-tenancy property (discussed below) or (2) tenancy in common property. Joint-tenancy property passes automatically to the surviving joint owner, tenancy in common property does *not:* It becomes part of the estate of the deceased. The clerk's office of the local courthouse may be able to give you some guidance as to what happens to tenancy-by-the-entirety property in your state in case of divorce.

Joint Tenancy. Joint tenancy differs from tenancy by the entirety in that joint-tenancy property isn't restricted to married people only. For example, with respect to real estate: if (1) an unmarried couple living together own their house in joint tenancy, or (2) business partners own their place of business in joint tenancy, then when one joint tenant dies, the other will own the house or business automatically. Again, this is called "right of survivorship." As you will see in the appendix, sometimes the deed has to refer specifically to a joint tenancy and/or the right of survivorship.

In some states, in addition to real estate, personal property such as shares of stock or bank accounts can be owned in joint tenancy. Once again, sometimes the document of ownership, such as the stock certificate or the bank agreement for a checking account, might have to refer specifically to a joint tenancy and/or the right of survivorship.

You may be thinking that joint tenancy sounds identical to tenancy by the entirety except for the fact that joint tenancy isn't limited to married people. However, not all states recognize both tenancy by the entirety and joint tenancy; some recognize one but not the other. There is no particularly good reason for this, but you must be prepared for it as you go through the appendix and if you consult the clerk's office of the local courthouse for further information. Further, some states recognize no type of tenancy-by-the-entirety property nor any type of joint-tenancy property: these states are usually *community-property states,* discussed further under Elective Rights below.

2. Intestate-share laws. If the deceased died intestate (remember, that means "without a will"), then state laws determine who gets what from the deceased's estate. These state laws are called intestate share laws. Intestate-share laws give the deceased's spouse, children, grandchildren, parents, or grandparents varying rights in the estate. Intestate-share laws can be complicated and the appendix only summarizes them, so be sure to consult with the local courthouse's clerk's office for guidance. For example, throughout the appendix you may note references to both *children* and *issue* of the deceased. The two are not identical: *issue* is a broader term because it includes grandchildren. Therefore, just one living grandchild who is all that's left of a family could inherit the intestate share reserved for *issue* under a state's intestate-share law if that is the term referred to in Appendix Two beginning on page 47.

> *Example."* Ross P. and Margot P. lived long, happy lives. They had two children, who in turn gave them eight grandchildren. Ross and Margot outlived their two children, but when Ross died, all eight grandchildren were still alive. Under the laws of state X, Ross's estate (worth billions) goes half to Margot and half to "'surviving issue," because Ross forgot to write his will. Who gets what?

> *Answer:* Margot gets half, and the eight grandchildren get 1/8 of the remaining half, or 1/16 of the total estate.

Example: Same as above, but Ross and Margot lived in state Y, which gives half of the estate of an intestate to the children, but no other descendants of the deceased. Who gets what?

Answer: Margot gets everything and the grandchildren get nothing.

Frequently, intestate-share laws split the deceased's estate among various surviving relatives. For example, the law might state that the deceased's spouse gets everything if there are no surviving children or parents of the deceased. However, the law may go on to say that if there are surviving parents and/or surviving children, the spouse usually gets a certain fixed dollar amount (anywhere from a few thousand dollars on up), and always gets one-half of the estate. Why just "usually" with respect to the dollar amount? Because it can vary depending on the number of surviving relatives and the nature of their relationship to the deceased.

In 1992, West Virginia became the first state to adopt certain recommended revisions to the Uniform Probate Code concerning a spouse's intestate share. These revisions provide that a spouse gets the entire estate if the deceased dies intestate, unless there are surviving descendants who are not the offspring of both the deceased and the surviving spouse (such as from previous marriages), or there are surviving parents of the deceased. More states will adopt these revisions in the future.

3. Elective rights. If the deceased was married when he or she died, and the living spouse is unhappy with what he or she was left under the will, then there are state laws concerning *elective rights.* The living spouse can refuse to accept what the will would leave him or her, and "elect" to take a portion of the estate provided by statute. These laws prevent the deceased from leaving the living spouse without means of support. For example, many state elective-rights statutes say that the spouse may elect to take up to one-third of the deceased's estate. Note that the spouse has a limited time period to assert his or her rights, which is done by filing a *notice of election* with the local courthouse. The spouse should consult with an attorney or the local courthouse's clerk's office concerning when the notice of election must be filed. If it isn't filed on time, the right to elect may be lost.

In 1992, West Virginia became the first state to adopt certain recommended revisions to the Uniform Probate Code concerning a spouse's elective rights. These revisions take a new approach to a spouse's elective share: The size of the elective share depends on how long the deceased and the spouse were married. The elective share percentage ranges from 3 percent if they were married for just a year to a maximum of 50 percent if they were married for fifteen years or more. More states will adopt these revisions in the future.

You will also see references throughout Appendix Two to *community property* and *separate property.* Some states have abolished tenancy by the entirety in favor of giving the surviving spouse the right to a specific share of all real estate and personal property acquired by the couple during their marriage. This is called *community property.* Sometimes the surviving spouse also has the right to property that the deceased brought into the marriage, such as cash or real estate acquired before getting married. This and certain and other types of property belonging to the deceased are called *separate property.*

The states that have adopted the community-property and separate-property approach are known generically as community-property states. Although these states have abolished tenancy by the entirety, they usually have not abolished joint tenancy. Check Appendix Two and the local courthouse's clerk's office for further details.

4. Automatic-share laws. In addition to intestate shares and elective rights, most states give the deceased's spouse the right to take a portion of the estate free of the claims of others. Although these laws are called "'automatic-share laws," don't confuse them with such automatic property-passing mechanisms as tenancy by the entirety or joint property. Whatever the spouse might be entitled to get ahead of other parties, it all comes out of the estate and is thus part of the assets subject to the court's supervision.

For example, a state's automatic-share law might give the spouse the right to (1) a *homestead exemption* of several thousand dollars, more or less, (2) a *personal-property* exemption of several thousand dollars, more or less, and (3) a court-approved allowance for family living expenses, which comes out of the estate. Normally you (the executor) won't have to do much more than obey the court's orders setting forth the spouse's automatic share, but you should at least familiarize yourself with your state's automatic-share principles as set forth in the appendix, just in case there is ever a legal dispute, such as with the deceased's creditors. Since the spouse's automatic share is typically not subject to *the* claims of *the* deceased's *creditors,* unlike *regular-estate* assets, you should contact the local courthouse's clerk's office if there is any question during your administration of the estate about creditors' rights.

Performing a legal audit of the estate

Once you've taken the four preliminary steps, especially determining the property of the estate and who holds certain important interests, you must perform a Legal Audit of the estate. As the executor, you are responsible for keeping track of all pertinent information concerning the estate. The form beginning on page 40 will assist you in performing the Legal Audit.

Fill in each and every item on the form as soon as possible after the date of death. When it is time for you to open the estate (see Chapter 3), the Legal Audit exercise will ensure that you are armed with the needed information. Further, you will find that the information you have collected will be invaluable in inventorying the estate, conducting appraisals, and performing the other duties of an executor.

Legal Audit

Date of this Legal Audit: _____

Dates of any revisions: _____ Which section/s: _____

_____   _____

_____   _____

I. The Assets.

Jointly-Owned Property. List all of the testator's property that is jointly owned and can thus be transferred automatically to the other owner. See Appendix Two concerning what forms of joint property ownership are permitted under the laws of the testator's state.

1. Real estate.

Address: (1) _____ (2) _____

_____   _____

_____   _____

Type of joint-property ownership:

(1) _____ (2) _____

Address: (3) _____ (4) _____

_____   _____

_____   _____

Type of joint-property ownership:

(3) _____ (4) _____

Do you have copies of relevant documents such as deeds, mortgages, leases, surveys, maps, property-tax assessments, appraisals, mortgage insurance, title insurance, second mortgages such as home-equity or improvement loans, and settlement documents?   __ Yes __ No

2. Valuable personal property, such as automobiles, furniture, appliances, rare stamps and coins, jewelry, works of art, and boats:

_____

_____

_____

Do you have copies of all relevant certificates of title, ownership agreements, and other proofs of ownership?   __ Yes __ No

3. Jointly-held bank accounts:

_____ Account number: _____

_____   _____

_____   _____

4. Jointly-held stocks and bonds:

_____ Certificate number: _____

_____   _____

_____   _____

5. Other jointly-owned property: _____

_____

_____

Non-Jointly-Owned Property.

1. List all real estate not jointly owned by the testator:

Address: (1) _____ (2) _____

_____ _____

Address: (3) _____ (4) _____

_____ _____

Do you have copies of relevant documents such as deeds, mortgages, leases, surveys, maps, property-tax assessments, appraisals, mortgage insurance, title insurance, second mortgages such as home-equity or improvement loans, and settlement documents?   __ Yes __No

2. List all valuable personal property such as automobiles, furniture, appliances, rare stamps and coins, jewelry, works of art, and boats:

_____

_____

Do you have copies of all relevant certificates of title and other proofs of ownership?   __ Yes __No

3. Bank accounts:

_____ Account number: _____

_____ _____

_____ _____

4. Stocks and bonds.

_____ Certificate number: _____

_____ _____

_____ _____

5. Did the testator have any business interests? If so, describe:

_____

_____

Do you have copies of any relevant partnership agreements, limited-partnership agreements, franchise agreements, or other documents concerning the testator's ownership rights in these business interests?   __ Yes __No

6. Other assets of the testator, such as debts due to him or her, royalties, trust benefits, and patents: _____

_____

_____

7. List the testator's liabilities, including all mortgages, deeds of trust, promissory notes, automobile loans, credit-card bills, hospital and doctor bills, vacation loans, and other personal debts:

Creditors: Loan/account number: Dollar amount:

_____   _____   _____

_____   _____   _____

_____   _____   _____

_____   _____   _____

_____   _____   _____

_____   _____   _____

_____   _____   _____

_____   _____   _____

8. Are there any lawsuits or other legal matters pending involving the testator or his assets and estate? If so, describe:_____

_____

_____

Do you have copies of the legal papers and the name and address of the attorney involved?   __ Yes __ No

Additional Items Not Subject to Estate Administration: Life Insurance and Trusts.

1. List the testator's life-insurance policies by company and policy number:

_____   Beneficiary   _____

_____   _____

_____   _____

Do you know who has possession of the policies?   __ Yes __ No

Did the testator have any loans, liens, or other debts secured by these life-insurance policies?   __ Yes __ No

2. List any trusts established by the testator:

Inter vivos trusts, or trusts set up during the testator's life:

     (1) Assets _____

           Beneficiary_____

           Trustee _____

           Special features _____

           Location of papers such as the Trust Agreement _____

     (2) Assets _____

           Beneficiary_____

           Trustee _____

           Special features _____

           Location of papers such as the Trust Agreement _____

(3) Assets _____

    Beneficiary _____

    Trustee _____

    Special features _____

    Location of papers such as the Trust Agreement _____

Testamentary trusts, or trusts that the will says must be set up now that the testator is dead:

(1) Assets _____

    Beneficiary _____

    Trustee Special features _____

    Location of papers such as the Trust Agreement _____

(2) Assets _____

    Beneficiary _____

    Trustee Special features _____

    Location of papers such as the Trust Agreement _____

(3) Assets _____

    Beneficiary _____

    Trustee Special features _____

    Location of papers such as the Trust Agreement _____

II. The Testator.

1. Date of death: _____

Do you have the death certificate? __ Yes __ No

2. Was the testator a U.S. citizen? __ Yes __ No

Do you have a copy of any citizenship papers? __ Yes __ No

If not a U.S. citizen, then a citizen of what country? _____

3. Testator's Social Security number: _____

4. Name of testator's spouse, if any: _____

        Address: _____

                 _____

        Phone: _____

Married in what state or country? _____

Did the testator have any previous spouses? __ Yes __ No

(1) Name: _____ Address: _____

                          _____

               Phone: _____

Married in what state or country: _____

Legal reason why the marriage terminated (death, divorce, separation):

_____

Date of termination: _____

(2) Name: _____ Address: _____

_____

Phone: _____

Married in what state or country: _____

Legal reason why the marriage terminated (death, divorce, separation):

_____

Date of termination: _____

5. Did the testator have any children?   __ Yes ___ No

Name/s: _____ Date/s of birth: _____

_____   _____

_____   _____

_____   _____

Were any children illegitimate, adopted, disinherited, or from previous marriages? If so, describe: _____

_____

If no children, list any living brothers, sisters, and parents:

Names: _____ Relationship: _____

_____   _____

_____   _____

_____   _____

_____   _____

6. Testator's date of birth: _____

Place of birth: _____

7. Did the testator serve in any of the armed forces of the United States?
__ Yes __ No

If so, do you have copies of the discharge papers and information on the testator's Veteran's Claim Number, Military Serial Number, and any military pension benefits?   __ Yes __ No

8. Who was the testator's employer? _____

Address: _____

_____

Phone: _____

Supervisor: _____

9. List all of the testator's benefit plans, including 401(k) and profit-sharing plans, pension plans, railroad-retirement benefits, labor union and other collective-bar-gaining benefits, and fraternal-order benefits: _____

_____

_____

10. Did the testator have any safe-deposit boxes, rent any self-storage units, or have any other places where documents and valuables could be found?

__ Yes __ No

If yes, do you have the keys or know the name and address of all persons with access? __ Yes __ No

III. The Will.

1. Is there a will? __ Yes __ No

Do you have the original? __ Yes __ No

If you don't have the original, do you have a copy? __ Yes __ No

What is the date of the will? _____

2. Are there any codicils, amendments, or other addendums to the will?

__ Yes __ No

What are the dates of such addendums? _____

3. Assuming that you are named the executor in the will, are any other persons designated to perform other functions?

Guardian/s: _____

Trustees: _____

Second or Ancillary Executors: _____

4. Who are the beneficiaries named in the will:

(1) _____ (2) _____ (3) _____

Address:

_____ _____ _____

_____ _____ _____

Phone: _____ _____ _____

5. Who are the witnesses to the will?

(1) _____ (2) _____ (3) _____

Address:

_____ _____ _____

_____ _____ _____

Phone: _____ _____ _____

6. Did a lawyer draft the will, or any addendums? __ Yes __ No

If so, what is his or her name? _____

Name of law firm: _____

Address: _____

_____

_____

Phone: _____

APPENDIX TWO

Fifty-state summary of forms of joint-property ownership, intestate-share laws, spousal right-of-election laws, and automatic-share laws. Includes the District of Columbia and the Virgin Islands. State laws change periodically, so be certain to confirm the information set forth below concerning your state with an authoritative source, such as the court clerk's office or if necessary an attorney.

ALABAMA

Forms of joint-property ownership:

There is no tenancy by the entirety. For real estate, joint ownership is presumed to be tenancy in common unless "right of survivorship or other words" indicating intent that surviving party own entire property are in the deed.

Any intestate-share law?

Yes. Spouse gets everything if deceased has no surviving children or parents. If there are surviving parents and/or surviving children, the spouse usually gets a certain fixed dollar amount and always gets half of the estate.

Any elective rights?

Yes. Spouse may elect to take up to one-third of the deceased's estate.

Any automatic-share law?

Yes. Homestead: $6,000. Personal property: $3,500. Allowance for family living expenses.

ALASKA

Forms of joint-property ownership:

Joint tenancy allowed for personal property only. Spouses are presumed to hold real estate by tenancy by the entirety unless the deed expressly says otherwise.

Any intestate-share law?

Yes. Spouse gets everything if deceased has no surviving children or parents. If there are surviving parents and/or surviving children, the spouse usually gets a certain fixed dollar amount and always gets one-half of the estate.

Any elective rights?

Yes. Spouse may take one-third of the estate.

Any automatic-share law?

Yes. Homestead: $27,000. Personal property: $10,000. Allowance for family living expenses if estate is insolvent.

ARIZONA

Forms of joint-property ownership:

There is no tenancy by the entirety for either real property or personal property. To create a joint tenancy between spouses in either real property or personal property, the deed or other document must clearly state that it is intended to be joint property with right of survivorship.

Any intestate-share law?

Yes. If the deceased had any children which were his or hers alone, such as from a previous marriage, the surviving spouse gets half of the deceased's "separate property" and half of the deceased's "community property." Otherwise, the surviving spouse takes all.

Any elective rights?

No.

Any automatic-share law?

Yes. Homestead: $12,000. Personal property: $7,000. Allowance for family living expenses. Half of all "community property."

ARKANSAS

Forms of joint-property ownership:

Tenancy by the entirety for both personal property and real property. Spouses are presumed to hold real estate by tenancy by the entirety unless the deed expressly says otherwise.

Any intestate-share law?

Yes. Spouse gets everything if there are no surviving children and was married to the deceased for more than three years. If there are no surviving children but spouse was married to deceased for less than three years, spouse gets half of the estate. If there are any surviving children the spouse gets no intestate share.

Any elective rights?

Yes. Arkansas has an intricate right-of-election statute tied into a spouse's "dower" or "courtesy" rights. Anyone considering exercising a right of election should consult a professional estate appraiser who is knowledgeable in this area and do so *quickly:* spouses have only one month after the claims filing deadline expires to use their right of election.

Any automatic-share law?

Yes. Homestead: $2,500. Personal property: $1,000. Half of all community property. Allowance for family living expenses of up to $500 for 2 months. Family furnishings.

CALIFORNIA

Forms of joint-property ownership:

There is no tenancy by the entirety for personal property or real property. Joint tenancy may be created, but only if the deed or other document expressly states that a joint tenancy with right of survivorship is intended.

Any intestate-share law?

Yes. Half of any property acquired during the marriage when and if the couple was not living in California. Depending upon the number and relationship of surviving family members, spouse also gets from one-third to all of the deceased's separate property.

Any elective rights?

No.

Any automatic-share law?

Yes. Spouse gets half of all property acquired during marriage, use of home for sixty days after filing inventory, and an allowance for family expenses.

COLORADO

Forms of joint-property ownership:

There is no tenancy by the entirety for either personal property or real property. Joint tenancies in both personal property and real property can be created, but the deed or other document should explicitly refer to a joint tenancy with right of survivorship.

Any intestate-share law?

Yes. Spouse gets everything if there are no surviving children. If any children are those of the deceased's only, such as from a prior marriage, the spouse gets half of the estate. If any children are also the spouse's, the spouse gets $25,000 and half of the rest of the estate.

Any elective rights?

Yes. Spouse may take half of the estate.

Any automatic-share law?

Yes. Half of all community property. Personal property: $7,500. Allowance for family living expenses if estate is insolvent.

CONNECTICUT

Forms of joint-property ownership:

There is no tenancy by the entirety for either personal property or real property. Joint tenancy in personal property and real property is recognized, and if the words "joint tenancy" are used in the deed or other document, then a right of survivorship is presumed to exist.

Any intestate-share law?

Yes. Spouse gets everything if the deceased leaves no surviving children and no surviving parents. Otherwise, depending on whether there are surviving children and/or surviving parents of the deceased, the spouse can get up to three-fourths of the estate plus the first $100,000.

Any elective rights?

Yes. Spouse can get a "lifetime use" of one-third of the estate.

Any automatic-share law?

Yes, but very limited. The court may allow for family living expenses and use of any family car during the administration of the estate.

DELAWARE

Forms of joint-property ownership:

Tenancy by the entirety recognized for both personal property and real property.

Any intestate-share law?

Yes. Spouse gets everything if the deceased has no surviving children and no surviving parents. Depending upon whether there are surviving parents and/or surviving children, the spouse may or may not get the first $50,000 of the estate, but will always get (1) half of the deceased's personal property, and (2) use of the deceased's real estate until the spouse dies.

Any elective rights?

Yes. Spouse may take one-third of the estate. The definition of "estate" is, however, tied to the definition of "adjusted gross estate," under federal estate tax law.

Any automatic-share law?

Yes, but very limited. There is a $2,000 allowance for living expenses.

DISTRICT OF COLUMBIA

Forms of joint-property ownership:

Tenancy by the entirety recognized for both personal property and real property.

Any intestate-share law?

Yes. Spouse gets everything if there are no surviving children of the spouse and/or the deceased and no surviving relatives or parents of the deceased. Otherwise, the spouse's intestate share will be from one-third to half of the deceased's estate.

Any elective rights?

Yes. Spouse can elect to take either (1) half of the deceased's estate, after debts, or (2) use of one-third of the deceased's real property until the spouse dies, and half of the deceased's other property, after debts.

Any automatic-share law?

Yes. Allowance for $10,000 in family living expenses, minus $750 in funeral costs.

FLORIDA

Forms of joint-property ownership:

Personal property and real property held by spouses is presumed to be tenancy by the entireties. Joint tenancy is recognized for both real property and personal property, but only if the deed or other document expressly refers to a "joint tenancy with right of survivorship."

Any intestate-share law?

Yes. Spouse gets everything if there are no surviving children. If there are any children, the spouse gets the first $20,000 and half of the rest of the estate. If any children are not those of the surviving spouse, such as from a prior marriage of the deceased, then the surviving spouse gets half of the estate.

Any elective rights?

Yes. Spouse may take 30 percent of the fair-market value of all estate property in Florida (excepting joint bank accounts and after mortgages or other liens.)

Any automatic-share law?

Yes. Household property: $10,000. Lifetime use of the spouse's real estate, $6,000 allowance for family living expenses during the administration of the estate, and $1,000 of the deceased's personal effects.

GEORGIA

Forms of joint-property ownership:

There is no tenancy by the entirety for real property or personal property. Joint tenancy is recognized for both real property and personal property if the deed or other document expressly refers to "joint tenancy with right of survivorship."

Any intestate-share law?

Yes. Spouse gets everything if there are no surviving children. If there are surviving children, the spouse and the children get equal shares of the estate, but the spouse always gets at least one fourth of the estate. Thus, if there are four or more children, they will have to divide the remaining three-fourths of the estate between themselves.

Any elective rights?

No.

Any automatic-share law?

Yes, but very limited. The court makes an allowance for family living expenses which starts at $1,600.

HAWAII

Forms of joint-property ownership:

Cars registered in two or more names are presumed to be held in joint tenancy. Other types of personal property and real property may be held in joint tenancy or tenancy by the entirety, but the deed or other document must expressly refer to a joint tenancy or tenancy by the entirety and should also refer to a "right of survivorship."

Any intestate-share law?

Yes. Spouse gets everything if there are no surviving children or parents of the deceased. If there are surviving parents and/or surviving children, the spouse gets half of the estate.

Any elective rights?

Yes. Spouse may take one-third of the estate in the deceased's will and one-third of any real estate not in the will, if owned by the deceased prior to July of 1977.

Any automatic-share law?

Yes. Homestead: $5,000. Personal property: $5,000. Allowance for family living expenses.

IDAHO

Forms of joint-property ownership:

Idaho is a community-property state. No tenancy by the entirety for real property or personal property. Joint tenancy recognized for both real property and personal property, but the deed or other document must expressly refer to a "joint tenancy with right of survivorship."

Any intestate-share law?

Yes. Spouse gets everything if there are no surviving children or parents of the deceased. If there are any surviving children who are not the spouse's, such as from a prior marriage of the deceased, the spouse gets half of the estate. In all other situations, the spouse gets half of the estate plus the first $50,000.

Any elective rights?

Yes. Half of any property acquired during the marriage when and if the couple was not living in Idaho.

Any automatic-share law?

Yes. Half of all community property. Homestead: $4,000, unless there are dependent children living with spouse, then $10,000. Personal property: $3,500. Allowance for living expenses during the administration.

ILLINOIS

Forms of joint-property ownership:

There is no tenancy by the entirety for real property or personal property. Joint tenancy is recognized for both real property and personal property, but the deed or other document must expressly state that the property is to be held by "joint tenancy with right of survivorship and not as tenants in common."

Any intestate-share law?

Yes. Spouse gets everything if there are no surviving children. If there are surviving children, the spouse gets half of the estate.

Any elective rights?

Yes. Spouse may take half of the estate if there are no surviving children. If there are surviving children, the spouse may take one-third of the estate.

Any automatic-share law?

Yes. Homestead: $7,500. Allowance for nine months of living expenses up to $10,000. Additional $2,000 for each dependent.

INDIANA

Forms of joint-property ownership:

Tenancy by the entirety not recognized for personal property. For some types of household goods acquired during the marriage and in the names of both spouses, such as cars and bonds, joint tenancy is presumed. Otherwise, personal property is held by joint tenancy only if the document expressly says so.

Spouses are presumed to hold real estate by tenancy by the entirety unless the deed expressly says otherwise. Real estate between unmarried persons can be held in joint tenancy, but only if the deed expressly refers to a joint tenancy.

Any intestate-share law?

Yes. Spouse gets everything if there are no surviving children or parents of the deceased. If there are surviving parents but no surviving children, the spouse gets three-fourths of the estate. If there are any surviving children, the spouse gets half of the estate. Special rules if surviving spouse is not deceased's first spouse.

Any elective rights?

Yes. Spouse may take half of the estate. Special rules if surviving spouse is not deceased's first spouse.

Any automatic-share law?

Yes, but very limited. Automatic share limited to $8,500 in personal property.

IOWA

Forms of joint-property ownership:

No tenancy by the entirety for real property or personal property. Joint tenancy is recognized for both real property and personal property, but the deed or other document must express an intent to create a joint tenancy.

Any intestate-share law?

Yes. Spouse gets everything if there are no surviving children who are children of the deceased only, such as from a prior marriage of the deceased. Otherwise, the spouse can get either the first $50,000 of the estate or half of the estate over $50,000.

Any elective rights?

Yes. Spouse may take one-third of the real estate owned by the deceased during the marriage and one third of the deceased's personal property. In the alternative, the spouse can elect to live in the family home for life.

Any automatic-share law?

Yes, but very limited. Spouse gets living expenses for one year and some personal property.

KANSAS

Forms of joint-property ownership:

No tenancy by the entirety for real property or personal property. Joint tenancy allowed for both real property and personal property, but the deed or other document must express intent that the property be held in joint tenancy.

Any intestate-share law?

Yes. Spouse gets everything if there are no surviving children. If there are surviving children, the spouse gets half of the estate.

Any elective rights?

Yes. Spouse can elect to take intestate share.

Any automatic-share law?

Yes. Personal property: $7,500. Spouse is also entitled to lifetime use of a certain amount of the deceased's real estate, which varies from one acre to 60 acres depending upon whether it is urban land or farmland.

KENTUCKY

Forms of joint-property ownership:

Tenancy by the entirety recognized for both real property and personal property, but the deed or other document must expressly state that the spouses own it as "tenants by the entirety" and should also say "with the right of survivorship." Joint tenancy is worthless, as there is no right of survivorship permitted for joint tenants.

Any intestate-share law?

Yes. Spouse gets everything if there are no surviving children, parents, or relatives of the deceased. Otherwise, the spouse's intestate share is simply what the spouse gets as his or her automatic share.

Any elective rights?

Yes, but for all practical purposes they are irrelevant, as they are virtually identical to the automatic share.

Any automatic-share law?

Yes, and very generous. Spouse gets half of all community property and half of the real estate owned by the deceased at death, plus lifetime use of one-third of other real estate. Further, the spouse gets half of the deceased's separate personal property and living expenses up to $7,500.

LOUISIANA

Forms of joint-property ownership:

Louisiana is a community-property state. Because Louisiana law is based on French civil law, it does not recognize tenancy by the entirety or joint tenancy for either real property or personal property.

Any intestate-share law?

Yes. Spouse gets everything if there are no surviving children or parents of the deceased. If there are surviving parents but no surviving children, spouse gets half of the estate. If there are any surviving children, spouse gets lifetime use of deceased's separate property, which terminates if spouse remarries.

Any elective rights?

No.

Any automatic-share law?

Yes. Spouse gets at least half the community property.

MAINE

Forms of joint-property ownership:

No tenancy by the entirety for real property or personal property. Joint tenancy in real property and personal property is recognized, but the deed or other document must expressly intend to create a joint tenancy and should also refer to a "right of survivorship."

Any intestate-share law?

Yes. Spouse gets everything if there are no surviving children or parents of the deceased. If there are surviving parents and/or surviving children, the spouse usually gets a certain fixed dollar amount and always gets half of the estate.

Any elective rights?

Yes. Spouse may take one-third of the estate.

Any automatic-share law?

Yes. Homestead: $5,000. Personal property: $3,500. Allowance for living expenses during term of estate administration and if estate is insolvent.

MARYLAND

Forms of joint-property ownership:

Spouses are presumed to own real property and personal property as tenants by the entirety. Joint tenancy is recognized for both real property and personal property, but the deed or other document must expressly state that the property is to be held in joint tenancy.

Any intestate-share law?

Yes. Spouse gets everything if there are no surviving children or parents of the deceased. If there are surviving parents and/or surviving children, the spouse usually gets a certain fixed dollar amount and always gets half of the estate.

Any elective rights?

Yes. Spouse may take half of the estate if there are no living children, one-third of the estate if there are living children. Spouse must file notice of election within 30 days after creditor claims are due.

Any automatic-share law?

Yes, but very limited. There is a $2,000 allowance for living expenses plus an additional $1,000 for every unmarried child under 18.

MASSACHUSETTS

Forms of joint-property ownership:

Joint tenancy and tenancy by the entirety recognized for both real property and personal property. Both forms of ownership require that the deed or other document expressly state that the property is to be held as joint tenants "with right of survivorship" or as tenants by the entirety "with right of survivorship."

Any intestate-share law?

Yes. Spouse gets everything if there are no surviving children, parents, or close relatives of the deceased. If there are no surviving children, but there are other surviving relatives, spouse gets the first $200,000 and half of anything over that amount. If there are surviving children, spouse gets half of the estate.

Any elective rights?

Yes. Spouse may take anywhere from one-third of the estate if there are surviving children, to $25,000 and half of the estate if there are no surviving children or relatives.

Any automatic-share law?

Yes. Homestead: use of anywhere from six months up to death or remarriage. Living expenses for six months.

MICHIGAN

Forms of joint-property ownership:

Tenancy by the entirety clearly recognized for real property only and is presumed to exist for real estate owned by spouses. Joint tenancy recognized for real property and personal property, but deed or other document must expressly declare the property to be in joint tenancy and should refer to "right of survivorship."

Any intestate-share law?

Yes. Spouse gets everything if there are no surviving children or parents of the deceased. If there are surviving parents and/or surviving children, the spouse usually gets a certain fixed dollar amount and always gets half of the estate.

Any elective rights?

Yes. Spouse may elect to take half of what he or she would have received if the deceased died intestate.

Any automatic-share law?

Yes. Homestead: $10,000. Personal property: $3,500. Allowance for living expenses.

MINNESOTA

Forms of joint-property ownership:

No tenancy by the entirety for real property or personal property. Joint tenancy allowed for real property and personal property if the deed or other document expressly declares the property to be in joint tenancy.

Any intestate-share law?

Yes. Spouse gets everything if there are no surviving children. If there are surviving children, the spouse usually gets a certain fixed dollar amount and always gets half of the estate.

Any elective rights?

Yes. Spouse may take one-third of the estate.

Any automatic-share law?

Yes. Personal property: $9,000 and one car. Use of homestead and allowance for living expenses.

MISSISSIPPI

Forms of joint-property ownership:

Tenancy by the entirety and joint tenancy recognized for both real property and personal property. Deed or other document must manifestly express an intent to create an estate in joint tenancy or entirety with the right of survivorship.

Any intestate-share law?

Yes. Spouse gets everything if there are no surviving children. If there are surviving children, the spouse and the children take equal shares of the estate.

Any elective rights?

Yes. Spouse may take one-third of the estate if there are surviving children, but no more than intestate share.

Any automatic-share law?

Yes. Homestead: lifetime use up to $30,000 and 150 acres. Allowance for living expenses.

MISSOURI

Forms of joint-property ownership:

Tenancy by the entirety presumed for real property and personal property of spouses. Joint tenancy recognized for real property and personal property, but deed or other document must expressly declare the property to be in joint tenancy.

Any intestate-share law?

Yes. Spouse gets everything if there are no surviving children or parents of the deceased. If there are surviving parents and/or surviving children, the spouse usually gets a certain fixed dollar amount and always gets half of the estate.

Any elective rights?

Yes. Spouse may take half of the estate if no surviving children. If there are surviving children, spouse may take one-third of the estate.

Any automatic-share law?

Yes. Homestead: $7,500 or up to half of estate, whichever is less. Some personal property and an allowance for living expenses.

MONTANA

Forms of joint-property ownership:

No tenancy by the entirety for either real property or personal property. Joint tenancy recognized for both real property and personal property, but the deed or other document must expressly declare that the property is to be held as a "joint interest."

Any intestate-share law?

Yes. Spouse gets everything if there are no surviving children who are children of the deceased's only, such as from a prior marriage. If there are surviving children of the deceased's only, the spouse gets from one-third to half of the estate.

Any elective rights?

Yes. Spouse may take one-third of the estate.

Any automatic-share law?

Yes. Homestead: up to $20,000. Personal property: up to $3,500. Allowance for living expenses.

NEBRASKA

Forms of joint-property ownership:

There is no tenancy by the entirety for either real property or personal property. Joint tenancy is recognized for both real property and personal property, but the deed or other document should expressly state that the property is owned "as joint tenants with right of survivorship."

Any intestate-share law?

Yes. Spouse gets everything if there are no surviving children or parents of the deceased. If there are surviving parents and/or surviving children, the spouse usually gets a certain fixed dollar amount and always gets half of the estate.

Any elective rights?

Yes. Spouse may take half of the estate.

Any automatic-share law?

Yes. Homestead: up to $7,500. Personal property: up to $5,000. Allowance for living expenses.

NEVADA

Forms of joint-property ownership:

Nevada is a community-property state. There is no tenancy by the entirety for either real property or personal property. Joint tenancy is recognized for both real property and personal property, but the deed or other document must expressly declare that the property is to be a joint tenancy.

Any intestate-share law?

Yes. Spouse gets all of the deceased's separate property if there are no surviving children, parents, brothers, or sisters. If there are any surviving children, parents, brothers, or sisters, the spouse gets from one-third to half of the deceased's separate property.

Any elective rights?

No.

Any automatic-share law?

Yes. In addition to half of the community property, the spouse gets a homestead exemption, some personal property, and possibly an allowance for living expenses.

NEW HAMPSHIRE

Forms of joint-property ownership:

There is no tenancy by the entirety for either real property or personal property. Joint tenancy is recognized for both real property and personal property, but the deed or other document must expressly state that the property is to be held "in joint tenancy with right of survivorship."

Any intestate-share law?

Yes. Spouse gets everything if there are no surviving children or parents of the deceased. If there are surviving parents and/or surviving children, the spouse usually gets a certain fixed dollar amount and always gets half of the estate.

Any elective rights?

Yes. Spouse may take one-third of the estate if there are surviving children. If there are no surviving children but there are surviving parents, brothers, or sisters, the spouse gets $20,000 and half of the rest of the estate. If there are no surviving children, parents, brothers, or sisters, the spouse gets $10,000—$2,000 for every year of marriage, and half of the rest of the estate.

Any automatic-share law?

Yes, but very limited. Spouse may use home for 40 days after death and gets an allowance for living expenses which will be deducted from his or her inheritance.

New Jersey

Forms of joint-property ownership:

Tenancy by the entirety recognized for both real property and personal property, but deed or other document must be explicit in naming both spouses as "husband and wife." Joint tenancy recognized for both real property and personal property, but deed or other document must expressly state intent to create joint tenancy.

Any intestate-share law?

Yes. Spouse gets everything if there are no surviving children or parents of the deceased. If there are surviving parents and/or surviving children, the spouse usually gets a certain fixed dollar amount and always gets half of the estate.

Any elective rights?

Yes. Spouse may take one-third of the estate.

Any automatic-share law?

Yes, but very limited. The spouse gets only an allowance for living expenses.

New Mexico

Forms of joint-property ownership:

Community-property state. There is no tenancy by the entirety for real property or personal property. Joint tenancy is recognized for real property, including real property owned by spouses, and personal property if the deed or other document expressly declares the property to be in joint tenancy.

Any intestate-share law?

Yes. Spouse gets everything if there are no surviving children. If there are any surviving children, spouse gets the deceased's half of all community property and one-fourth of the deceased's separate property.

Any elective rights?

No.

Any automatic-share law?

Yes. Half of all community property. Homestead: up to $100,000. Personal property: $3,500. $10,000 allowance for living expenses.

NEW YORK

Forms of joint-property ownership:

Tenancy by the entirety allowed for real property only. Spouses are presumed to hold real estate by tenancy by the entirety unless the deed expressly says otherwise. Joint tenancy is recognized for both real property and personal property but only if the deed or other document expressly refers to the property as being owned in joint tenancy.

Any intestate-share law?

Yes. Spouse gets everything if there are no surviving children or parents of the deceased. If there are surviving parents and/or surviving children, the spouse gets the first $4,000 to $25,000 of the estate and from one-third to half of the rest.

Any elective rights?

Yes. Spouse may take from one-third to half of the estate.

Any automatic-share law?

Yes, but very limited. Personal property: up to $6,000.

NORTH CAROLINA

Forms of joint-property ownership:

Tenancy by the entirety allowed for real property only. Joint tenancy is recognized for both real property and personal property, but the deed or other document must expressly state that the property is to be held as "joint tenants with right of survivorship."

Any intestate-share law?

Yes. Spouse gets everything if there are no surviving children or parents of the deceased. If there are surviving parents and/or surviving children, the spouse gets from $15,000 to $25,000 in personal property and one third to half of the balance of the estate.

Any elective rights?

Yes. If the provision for the spouse in the will is less than what the spouse would have received as his or her intestate share if the deceased had died intestate, the spouse may elect to take one-third of the real estate owned during the marriage or have use of the deceased's home for the spouse's lifetime.

Any automatic-share law?

Yes. Allowance for family living expenses from $5,000 to half of the deceased's annual income prior to date of death.

NORTH DAKOTA

Forms of joint-property ownership:

Tenancy by the entirety not recognized for either real property or personal property. Joint tenancy is recognized for both real property and personal property, but the deed or other document must expressly intend to create a joint tenancy and should refer to a "right of survivorship."

Any intestate-share law?

Yes. Spouse gets everything if there are no surviving children or parents of the deceased. If there are surviving parents and/or surviving children, the spouse usually gets a certain fixed dollar amount and always gets half of the estate.

Any elective rights?

Yes. Spouse may take one-third of the estate.

Any automatic-share law?

Yes. Spouse gets use of homestead for his or her lifetime. Personal property: $5,000. Allowance for family living expenses.

Ohio

Forms of joint-property ownership:

Tenancy by the entirety recognized for real property but not for personal property. Joint tenancy recognized for both real property and personal property, but it is referred to as a "survivorship tenancy." Check with clerk's office of local court as to requirements for any specific language in deed or other document.

Any intestate-share law?

Yes. Spouse gets everything if there are no surviving children. If there are surviving children, spouse gets from the first $20,000 to the first $60,000 of the estate, and from one-third to half of the balance of the estate.

Any elective rights?

Yes. Spouse may elect to take what he or she would have received if the deceased died intestate.

Any automatic-share law?

Yes, but limited. Spouse gets use of homestead for one year and $5,000 allowance for living expenses. Living expenses are deducted from spouse's inheritance.

Oklahoma

Forms of joint-property ownership:

Tenancy by the entirety recognized for both real property and personal property. Joint tenancy recognized for both real property and personal property if the deed or other document expressly refers to a "joint tenancy with right of survivorship."

Any intestate-share law?

Yes. Spouse gets everything if there are no surviving children, parents, brothers, or sisters of the deceased. If there are surviving children, parents, brothers, or sisters, the spouse gets from half to all of the property acquired by "joint industry" during the marriage and from up to half of the estate.

Any elective rights?

Yes. Spouse may take up to one-fourth of the estate.

Any automatic-share law?

Yes. Use of homestead, some personal property, and an allowance for living expenses.

OREGON

Forms of joint-property ownership:

Tenancy by the entirety is recognized for real property but not for personal property. Equivalent of joint tenancy is recognized for real property and personal property if the deed or other document expressly states that the property is to be held "not as tenants in common but with the right of survivorship."

Any intestate-share law?

Yes. Spouse gets everything if there are no surviving children who are children of the deceased's only, such as from a prior marriage. If there are any surviving children who are children of the deceased's only, the spouse gets half of the estate.

Any elective rights?

Yes. Spouse may take one-fourth of the estate.

Any automatic-share law?

Yes. Use of homestead for one year and allowance for living expenses of up to two years.

PENNSYLVANIA

Forms of joint-property ownership:

Tenancy by the entirety recognized for both real property and personal property. Spouses are presumed to hold real estate by tenancy by the entirety unless the deed expressly says otherwise. Joint tenancy is recognized for both real property and personal property but only if the deed or other document expressly states that the property is to be held as a "joint tenancy with right of survivorship."

Any intestate-share law?

Yes. Spouse gets everything if there are no surviving children or parents of the deceased. If there are surviving parents and/or surviving children, the spouse usually gets a certain fixed dollar amount and always gets half of the estate.

Any elective rights?

Yes. Spouse may take one-third of the estate.

Any automatic-share law?

Yes, but very limited. There is an allowance for up to $2,000 in living expenses.

RHODE ISLAND

Forms of joint-property ownership:

Tenancy by the entirety recognized for both real property and personal property. Joint tenancy recognized for both real property and personal property, but the deed or other document must expressly declare that a joint tenancy is created and should refer to a "right of survivorship."

Any intestate-share law?

Yes. Spouse gets $50,000 in personal property, up to $75,000 in real estate and lifetime use of the rest of the real estate, and half of the balance of the estate if there are no surviving children. If there are surviving children, the spouse gets only half of the deceased's personal property.

Any elective rights?

Yes. Spouse may elect to use all of the estate's real estate for his or her lifetime.

Any automatic-share law?

Yes. Some personal property and a six-month allowance for family living expenses.

SOUTH CAROLINA

Forms of joint-property ownership:

There is no tenancy by the entirety for either real property or personal property. Joint tenancy recognized for real property and some types of personal property, not including stocks and bonds, if the deed or other document expressly states that the property is to be held in joint tenancy "with right of survivorship."

Any intestate-share law?

Yes. Spouse gets everything if there are no surviving children. If there are any surviving children, the spouse gets half of the estate.

Any elective rights?

Yes. Spouse may take one-third of the estate.

Any automatic-share law?

Yes. Some personal property and $5,000.

SOUTH DAKOTA

Forms of joint-property ownership:

There is no tenancy by the entirety for either real property or personal property. Joint tenancy is recognized for both real property and personal property, but the deed or other document must expressly create a joint tenancy.

Any intestate-share law?

Yes. Spouse gets everything if there are no surviving children, parents, brothers, sisters, nephews, or nieces of the deceased. Otherwise, spouse usually gets one-third of the estate to $100,000 and half of the balance of the estate.

Any elective rights?

Yes. Spouse may elect to take $100,000 or one-third of the estate, whichever is greater.

Any automatic-share law?

Yes. Lifetime use of homestead. Personal property: up to $1,500. Allowance for family living expenses.

TENNESSEE

Forms of joint-property ownership:

Tenancy by the entirety is recognized for both real property and personal property. Joint tenancy is recognized for both real property and personal property, but only if the deed or other document expressly intends to create a joint tenancy and refers to a "right of survivorship."

Any intestate-share law?

Yes. Spouse gets everything if there are no surviving children. If there are surviving children, the spouse can divide the estate equally with the children or take one-third of the estate, whichever is larger.

Any elective rights?

Yes. Spouse may elect to retain his or her interest in any community property.

Any automatic-share law?

Yes. Homestead: $5,000. Allowance for living expenses.

TEXAS

Forms of joint-property ownership:

Community-property state. There is no tenancy by the entirety for either real property or personal property. Joint tenancy allowed for real property if the deed or other document expressly creates a joint tenancy and refers to a "right of survivorship."

Any intestate-share law?

Yes. Spouse gets everything if there are no surviving children, parents, brothers, sisters, nieces, or nephews of the deceased. Otherwise, the spouse gets half of the community property and certain portions of the deceased's separate property.

Any elective rights?

No.

Any automatic-share law?

Yes. Half of all community property. Lifetime use of homestead as well as some personal property, additional real-estate acreage, and an allowance for living expenses.

UTAH

Forms of joint-property ownership:

Tenancy by the entirety clearly recognized for real property only. Joint tenancy recognized for real property and personal property, but only if the deed or other document expressly creates a joint tenancy.

Any intestate-share law?

Yes. Spouse gets everything if there are no surviving children who are children of the deceased only, such as from a prior marriage. If there are any children who are children of the deceased only, the spouse gets half of the estate.

Any elective rights?

Yes. Spouse may take one-third of the estate.

Any automatic-share law?

Yes. Homestead: $10,000. Personal property: $5,000. Up to $25,000 in automobiles, but no more than four automobiles. Allowance for family living expenses.

VERMONT

Forms of joint-property ownership:

Tenancy by the entirety recognized for both real property and personal property. Joint tenancy recognized for both real property and personal property, but the deed or other document must expressly create a joint tenancy.

Any intestate-share law?

Yes. Spouse gets everything if there are no surviving children or other relatives of the deceased. If there are no surviving children but there are surviving relatives, the spouse gets $25,000 and half of the rest of the estate. If there are surviving children, the spouse gets one-third of the estate's personal property and one-third to half of the estate's real estate.

Any elective rights?

Yes. Spouse's right of election is from one-third to half of the estate, depending on the number of surviving children.

Any automatic-share law?

Yes. Homestead: $30,000. Allowance for family living expenses.

VIRGIN ISLANDS

Forms of joint-property ownership:

Tenancy by the entirety clearly recognized for real property only, and spouses are presumed to hold real estate by tenancy by the entirety unless the deed expressly says otherwise. Joint tenancy recognized for both real property and personal property, but only if the deed or other document expressly creates a joint tenancy.

Any intestate-share law?

Yes. Spouse gets everything if there are no surviving children, parents, brothers, sisters, nephews, or nieces of the deceased. Otherwise, the spouse usually gets from $5,000 to $10,000 and always gets from one-third to half of the estate.

Any elective rights?

Yes. Spouse may take up to half of the estate.

Any automatic-share law?

Yes, but very limited. Court determines a homestead and living allowance for the spouse.

Virginia

Forms of joint-property ownership:
Tenancy by the entirety recognized for both real property and personal property. Joint tenancy recognized for both real property and personal property, but only if the deed or other document expressly creates a joint tenancy and refers to a "right of survivorship."

Any intestate-share law?
Yes. Spouse gets everything if there are no surviving children who are children of the deceased's only, such as from a prior marriage. If there are any children who are children of the deceased only, the spouse gets one-third of the estate.

Any elective rights?
Yes. Spouse may take half of the estate if there are no surviving children. If there are any surviving children, the spouse gets one-third of the estate.

Any automatic-share law?
Yes, but limited. Homestead: $5,000. Personal property: $3,500. Allowance for family living expenses.

Washington

Forms of joint-property ownership:
Community-property state. Technically, tenancy by the entirety is recognized for both real property and personal property, but it is worthless as no right of survivorship is included. Joint tenancy, however, is recognized for both real property and personal property if the deed or other document expressly creates a joint tenancy and refers to a "right of survivorship."

Any intestate-share law?
Yes, and very generous. Surviving spouse always gets all of the community property, which usually will be the bulk of the estate. If there are any surviving parents and/or children, they may be entitled to from one-fourth to half of the deceased's separate property, if any.

Any elective rights?
No.

Any automatic-share law?
Yes. Half of all community property and an allowance for living expenses. Spouse may also be entitled to take an additional $30,000 in homestead allowance and personal property.

West Virginia

Forms of joint-property ownership:
Tenancy by the entirety and joint tenancy recognized for both real property and personal property, but the deed or other document must expressly create such a tenancy and must refer to a "right of survivorship."

Any intestate-share law?

Yes. Spouse gets everything, unless there are surviving descendants who are not the offspring of both the deceased and the surviving spouse (such as from previous marriages), or there are surviving parents of the deceased.

Any elective rights?

Yes. Spouse may take a percentage of the estate based on the length of the marriage. The percentage begins at 3 percent if married for only one year, and reaches 50 percent if married for fifteen years or more.

Any automatic-share law?

Yes. Use of homestead and $1,000 in personal property.

WISCONSIN

Forms of joint-property ownership:

There is no tenancy by the entirety for either real property or personal property. Joint tenancy is recognized for both real property and personal property, and spouses are presumed to hold real estate by joint tenancy unless the deed expressly says otherwise.

Any intestate-share law?

Yes. Spouse gets everything if there are no surviving children who are children of the deceased's only, such as from a prior marriage. If there are surviving children who are children of the deceased's only, the spouse gets half of the estate.

Any elective rights?

No.

Any automatic-share law?

Yes. Half of all community property acquired from January 1, 1986 to date of death. Homestead: $10,000. Personal property: $1,000. Allowance for family living expenses.

WYOMING

Forms of joint-property ownership:

Tenancy by the entirety recognized for both real property and personal property. Joint tenancy recognized for both real property and personal property, but the deed or other document should expressly create a joint tenancy and refer to a "right of survivorship."

Any intestate-share law?

Yes. Spouse gets everything if there are no surviving children. If there are any surviving children, the spouse gets half of the estate.

Any elective rights?

Yes. Spouse may elect to take from one-fourth, to half of the estate, depending on whether or not there are surviving children.

Any automatic-share law?

Yes. Homestead: Up to $30,000. Some personal property. Allowance for family living expenses.

OPENING THE ESTATE

Now that you have completed all of the preliminary steps outlined in Chapters 1 and 2, you are finally ready to initiate the first necessary legal step in estate administration. This step is called "opening the estate," the process by which the state court supervises and approves your administration of the estate.

You must contact the state court for the city or county where the deceased had his or her legal residence and ask how to go about opening the estate. If you are uncertain about where to go, call directory assistance for the telephone number of the deceased's local courthouse. Once you've reached the courthouse, ask for the clerk's office where estates are administered. Usually estate administration is just another part of the normal bureaucratic functioning of the local courthouse. Depending on your state, you may encounter unique or archaic titles for the particular branch of the local courthouse that handles estates: for example, Court of Chancery, Register of Wills, Probate Court, or Orphans' Court. These titles are just labels, however, and are nothing to cause you concern.

Once you've found out where to go, understand that every state has its own rules, regulations, and forms concerning opening the estate. Most states, however, provide that you can open the estate as either (1) a *regular estate* or (2) a *small estate*. A regular estate means complying with all of the state's procedural requirements and restrictions, such as the notice-to-creditors requirement discussed later in this chapter and outlined by state in this chapter's appendix. A small estate, however, has much simpler procedures and takes less time.

Remember Chapters 1 and 2 and the discussions on good estate planning and the use of joint property to pass assets outside of the estate. Now consider the following hypothetical situations:

Example. Elvis dies and leaves his entire estate to his wife, Priscilla. Elvis and Priscilla had $100,000,000 in tenancy-by-the-entirety real estate and $50,000,000 in tenancy-by-the-entirety personal property. Elvis's only other assets were $10,000 in sequin suits, owned in his own name only. In Elvis's state, State X, his executor can open Elvis's estate as a small estate if Elvis's estate is less than $25,000. Can the executor open Elvis's estate as a small estate in State X?

Answer. Yes. The only assets in Elvis's estate are the $10,000 in sequin suits, so his executor can open the estate as a small estate in State X because it is worth less than $25,000.

Example. Homer dies and leaves his entire estate to his wife, Marge. Homer and Marge owned no tenancy-by-the-entirety or joint property, and they rented, rather than owned, their home. Homer's only asset was a mattress stuffed with $30,000 in cash, representing Homer's life savings. Homer also lives in State X, so Homer's executor can open Homer's estate as a small estate if Homer's estate is less than $25,000. Can the executor open Homer's estate as a small estate in State X?

Answer. No. Homer's estate is worth $30,000 and therefore cannot be opened as a small estate.

The lesson of these two hypothetical scenarios is that it doesn't matter what the deceased's wealth was, it's what's in the estate that matters in opening a small estate. Further, to open a small estate, it usually doesn't matter if the deceased had a will or died intestate.

A final word about opening small estates

The appendix to this chapter mentions notice to creditors: these requirements don't always apply to small estates. Further, some of the state laws summarized in the appendices to other chapters may also not apply to small estates. Check with the local courthouse for details. The clerk's office may also be able to provide you with a booklet or pamphlet that describes the locality's small-estate requirements.

Further, note that the definition of a small estate may not be as clear-cut as in the hypothetical State X. As you will see in the appendix, a state might define a small estate in such terms as "an estate worth less than the sum of (1) the spouse's exemptions, plus (2) administrative costs, deceased's last-illness expenses, and funeral expenses." If your state is such a state, you should (1) call the local courthouse to see if they can help you further, and (2) consult Chapters 2 and 5 for help. The exemptions referred to are usually the automatic-share laws described in Chapter 2, and the costs and expenses referred to are usually creditor claims given priority under state law as described in Chapter 5.

Filing the forms to open the estate

You may be able to get the court to mail you the necessary forms, although sometimes the court requires you to pick them up in person. Again, there are differences among the states, but whether it is a regular estate or a small estate, the most important difference among the forms are those required for *Letters Testamentary* versus those required for *Letters of Administration.*

Letters means the court order approving you as the executor of the will. Letters Testamentary is that court order for deceased persons who had a will. Letters of Administration is that court order for deceased persons who died intestate. Tell the clerk's office which type of Letters you are applying for, and ask for the proper forms. The forms require you to provide any one or more of the following:

1. The original or a copy of the will.

2. The original or a copy of the death certificate.

3. Information such as the names and addresses of the witnesses to the will, which you will have if you completed the Legal Audit.

4. An insurance bond, which acts to protect the beneficiaries of the will and other third parties should you fail to carry out your duties properly as executor.

5. A list of persons with an interest in the estate, which can be either (a) the beneficiaries named in the will, or (b) if the deceased is intestate, the spouse, children, and perhaps certain other relatives.

6. A preliminary inventory, summarizing the value of the estate's assets. Again, remember the importance of thoroughly completing the Legal Audit.

7. A list of all known creditors of the deceased. You will be required to look diligently for all such creditors, so have the deceased's records at hand.

8. A list of all the deceased's real estate and valuable personal property interests.

9. If the deceased was intestate, your solemn affirmation that you diligently searched for any will that the deceased might have.

10. Personal information concerning you, such as whether you have a criminal record or a history of mental illness.

After you have properly completed and filed all of the necessary forms with the court, the court should mail you the Letters you requested within a couple days or weeks. If there is a problem with the documents you filed, the clerk's office will probably call or write you. If you haven't heard from the court or the clerk's office within a month after you filed your forms, however, you should call them and find out what the delay is.

Getting your letters: A summary

1. Can you open the estate as a small estate? Check this chapter's appendix and call the local courthouse. If yes, go to point 2 below. If no, go to point 4 below.

2. Did the deceased have a will? If yes, fill out the small-estate forms required to get your Letters Testamentary. If no, go to point 3 below.

3. Fill out the small-estate forms required to get your Letters of Administration.

4. Did the deceased have a will? If yes, fill out the regular-estate forms required to get your Letters Testamentary. If no, go to point 5 below.

5. Fill out the regular-estate forms required to get your Letters of Administration.

When you receive your Letters, it will probably be a simple, one-page form that looks something like the sample Letters on pages 75 and 76.

Of course, there is always the possibility that the court will refuse to grant your request for Letters. The most common reasons for refusal are: (1) failing to file all the required forms, (2) filing incomplete forms, and (3) failing to meet the state's qualification requirements for executors, covered in Chapter 1. Reasons (1) and (2) should be easy to correct: after you complete the forms or portions of forms that you missed before, the court will probably give you the Letters.

Reason (3), however, may not be so easy. If you have been denied Letters for some specific reason such as being a nonresident or having a felony on your criminal record, there is probably very little you can do. Ask the local courthouse's clerk's office about filing an appeal or requesting a special exception. You may have no choice, however, other than to (a) hire a lawyer to contest the denial of Letters, or (b) give up. If you have been denied Letters for a nonspecific reason, such as "being deemed unsuitable," you may have a better chance in winning if you appeal, request an exception, or fight the denial.

If there are any minors, is there a legal guardian?

If the deceased had any children who are minors, the court must appoint a legal guardian. Guardians have different responsibilities from executors: guardians see to the education, health, and welfare of the deceased's children and are responsible for the safekeeping and prudent investment of the children's share of the estate until the children become adults.

If you want to be the children's guardian as well as the estate executor, as most surviving spouses do, first take a look at the will. There should be a clause in the will that reads something like this:

> If any one or more of my children shall be minors at the time of my death, I nominate and appoint _____ of _____ , State of _____ , to be the Guardian of the person of my minor child or children. In the event that at any time and for any reason fails to become or ceases to be Guardian hereunder, I nominate and appoint _____ of __ , State of _____ , to be the Successor Guardian of the person of my minor child or children.

In the sample will included in Chapter 1 this clause is Article Tenth, but it can be anywhere in the will and still be valid. You or any other person named as the guardian must contact the deceased's local courthouse and find out what forms and procedures are involved: they could be different from what you went through to become executor. If the will doesn't have a guardianship clause, or the deceased died intestate, then the process may become more time-consuming while the court determines the best interests of the children in considering any guardianship application.

Now that you're an executor:
Issuing formal notices to creditors.

Your most important initial duty after receiving your Letters is to issue the formal notice of the deceased's death required by law to the deceased's creditors. "Creditors" includes any person or business that the deceased owed money to: credit-card companies, utilities, doctors, hospitals, car-finance companies, banks, and so forth. You may have already contacted some of these creditors during the preliminary steps discussed in Chapters 1 and 2. Nevertheless, you still have to give the formal legal notice.

Why is giving legal notice important? Because after receiving legal notice, creditors have a limited time period to file a statement with the court saying what the deceased owed them. If they don't file the required statement, the creditors lose their claim and the right to collect the debt. If this happens, there may be more money left in the estate for the beneficiaries. If notice isn't given, however, the creditor(s) may have much longer, even several years, to collect debts from the estate.

This chapter's appendix also summarizes state laws concerning the legal notice you are required to give creditors. Because creditors have at least a couple of months to file their statements with the court, creditor deadlines are not included in this chapter's appendix but are in Appendix Five on page 111. Chapter 5 specifically discusses your duty to pay off claims against the estate.

The following represents a typical state notice requirement:

> The executor must notify known creditors of appointment and must see that a notice is published once a week for three straight weeks in a local newspaper.

By "notice," the law means a specific form, which you can obtain from the local courthouse.

The notice requirement sounds easy enough, but let's analyze, piece by piece, what it requires you to do. This analysis will help you understand the process better and avoid mistakes in complying with your state's requirements.

1. "The executor must notify known creditors of appointment..." Check with the courthouse, but usually this phrase means that you must mail a copy of the notice to all of the deceased's creditors. This is called "actual notice," as opposed to "notice by publication," discussed in point 2. Let me add that you must make a diligent effort to mail *all* creditors and thus give them all actual notice.

   Even if the law doesn't require actual notice for all creditors, some state courts are beginning to hold that the Constitution's due-process clause requires actual notice to all creditors. This area of the law is still developing, and as of this date only a few courts have held that state-law limitations on filing claims don't apply if creditors don't get actual notice. However, I believe that more and more courts will require executors to give actual notice to all creditors. Therefore, my advice to you is to give actual notice to all of the deceased's creditors whether or not state law requires it. If you have a thorough Legal Audit and the deceased's books and records, this shouldn't be too hard to accomplish.

2. "...and must see that a notice is published once a week for three straight weeks in a local newspaper." In addition to mailing out notices, a copy of the notice must be published in a newspaper that circulates in the deceased's locality. This is the "notice by publication" discussed in point 1. Sometimes it's not actually the executor who handles publishing the notice to creditors, but the clerk's office of the local courthouse on the executor's behalf. You should check periodically with the clerk's office to make sure that they have published the notice as required by law. After all, you, not the clerk's office, are ultimately responsible for proper estate administration.

State of Maryland
LETTERS OF ADMINISTRATION

Estate No. _____

I certify that administration of the Estate of

_____

was granted on the _____ day of _____, 200 _____

to _____

as personal representative and the appointment is in effect

this _____ day of _____, 200 _____

SAMPLE

❏ Will probated _____
                          (date)

❏ Intestate estate.

_____
Register of Wills

_____

RW 20   VALID ONLY IF SEALED WITH THE SEAL OF THE COURT OR THE REGISTER

State of Maryland
LETTERS OF ADMINISTRATION OF SMALL ESTATE

Estate No. _____

I certify that administration of the Estate of

_____

was granted on the _____ day of _____ , 200 ____

to _____

as personal representative and the appointment is in effect

this _____ day of _____ , 200 ____

❑ Will probated _____
                          (date)

❑ Intestate estate.

_____
Register of Wills for

_____

VALID ONLY IF SEALED WITH THE SEAL OF THE COURT OR THE REGISTER

RW 7

(FILE IN DUPLICATE)

_____

_____

_____

(name and address of personal representative or attorney)

NOTICE OF APPOINTMENT
NOTICE TO CREDITORS   Estate No. _____
NOTICE TO UNKNOWN HEIRS

TO ALL PERSONS INTERESTED IN THE ESTATE OF _____

Notice is given that _____
                                    (name and address)

_____ was on _____
                                                              (date)

appointed personal representative of the estate of _____

who died on _____ (with)   (without) a will.
                    (date)

There was a prior small estate proceeding. (Delete last sentence if inapplicable).

Further information can be obtained by reviewing the estate file in the office of the Register of Wills or by contacting the personal representative or the attorney.

All persons having any objection to the appointment (or to the probate of the decedent's will) shall file their objections with the Register of Wills on or before the _____ day of _____ 200_____ .
                                                                            (6 months from date of appointment)

(The above paragraph shall be deleted where the initial appointment of a personal representative is made under judicial probate.)

Any person having a *claim against* the decedent must present the claim to the undersigned personal representative or file it with the Register of Wills with a copy to the undersigned on or before the earlier of the following dates:

(1)   Nine months from the date of the decedent's death: or

(2)   Two months after the personal representative mails or otherwise delivers to the creditor a copy of this published notice or other written notice notifying the creditor that the claim will be barred unless the creditor presents the claims within two months from the mailing or other delivery of the notice. A claim not presented or filed on or before that date, or any extension provided by law, is unenforceable thereafter. Claim forms may be obtained from the Register of Wills.

_____

_____

_____

Personal Representative(s)

True Test Copy

Name and Address of Register of Wills for

_____

_____

Name of newspaper designated by personal representative: _____

PUBLISH THREE TIMES

RW 14

Appendix Three

Fifty-state-summary of notice requirements to creditors and availability of simplified rules for small estates. Also includes the District of Columbia and the Virgin Islands. State laws change periodically, so be certain to confirm the information set forth below concerning your state with an authoritative source, such as the court clerk's office or if necessary an attorney.

NOTICE REQUIREMENTS TO CREDITORS:	ARE THERE SIMPLIFIED RULES FOR SMALL ESTATES?
ALABAMA	
Must notify known creditors of appointment within one month after getting appointed. Further, within a month after appointment the executor must see that a notice is published once a week, for three straight weeks, in a local newspaper.	Yes, for estates consisting only of personal property worth less than $3,000.
ALASKA	
Must notify known creditors of appointment and must see that a notice is published once a week, for three straight weeks, in a local newspaper.	Yes, for estates worth less than $15,000.

NOTICE REQUIREMENTS TO CREDITORS:	ARE THERE SIMPLIFIED RULES FOR SMALL ESTATES?
ARIZONA	
Must notify known creditors of appointment and must see that a notice is published once a week, for three straight weeks, in a local newspaper.	Yes, for estates worth less than $30,000.
ARKANSAS	
Must notify known creditors of appointment and must see that a notice is published once a week, for two straight weeks, in a local newspaper. If the estate is worth less than $1,000, executor only has to post notice in the courthouse.	Yes, for estates worth less than $50,000.
CALIFORNIA	
Before being appointed, executor must publish notice once a week, for three straight weeks, in a local newspaper. After appointment, executor must also notify known creditors within four months or within 30 days of discovering a new creditor, whichever is later.	Yes, for estates where the total value of all real and personal property in California is less than $60,000.
COLORADO	
Must notify known creditors of appointment and must see that a notice is published once a week, for three straight weeks, in a local newspaper.	Yes, for estates worth less than $27,000.
CONNECTICUT	
The court determines what the executor must do to notify creditors on a case-by-case basis.	Yes, for estates worth less than $20,000.
DELAWARE	
Must notify known creditors of appointment and, within 40 days of appointment, the executor must see that notice is published once a week, for three straight weeks, in a local newspaper.	Yes, for estates worth less than $12,500.

| NOTICE REQUIREMENTS TO CREDITORS: | ARE THERE SIMPLIFIED RULES FOR SMALL ESTATES? |

DISTRICT OF COLUMBIA

Must notify known creditors of appointment and, within 20 days after appointment, see that notice is published once a week, for three straight weeks, in the *Washington Law Reporter* and any other publication ordered by the court.

Yes, for estates worth less than $10,000.

FLORIDA

Must notify known creditors of appointment and must see that a notice is published once a week, for two straight weeks, in a local newspaper.

Yes, for estates worth less than $60,000.

GEORGIA

Must notify known creditors of appointment, and within 60 days must see that a notice is published once a week, for four straight weeks, in a local newspaper.

No.

HAWAII

Must notify known creditors of appointment and must see that a notice is published once a week, for three straight weeks, in a local newspaper.

Yes, for estates worth less than $20,000.

IDAHO

Must notify known creditors of appointment and must see that a notice is published once a week, for three straight weeks, in a local newspaper.

Yes, for estates worth less than $5,000.

ILLINOIS

Must notify known creditors of appointment and, within two weeks of appointment, must see that a notice is published once a week, for three straight weeks, in a local newspaper.

Yes, for estates worth less than $50,000.

NOTICE REQUIREMENTS TO CREDITORS:	ARE THERE SIMPLIFIED RULES FOR SMALL ESTATES?
INDIANA	
Must notify known creditors of appointment and must see that a notice is published once a week, for two straight weeks, in a local newspaper.	Yes, for estates worth less than $15,000.
IOWA	
Must notify known creditors of appointment and must see that a notice is published once a week, for two straight weeks, in a local newspaper.	Yes, for estates worth less than $50,000.
KANSAS	
Must notify known creditors of appointment and, within 10 days of filing petition for letters, must see that a notice is published once a week, for three straight weeks, in a local newspaper.	Yes, for estates with no real estate and where the assets are worth less than the claims allowed by Law 59-1301.
KENTUCKY	
Must notify known creditors of appointment and must see that clerk of court publishes notice of appointment at least once in a local newspaper.	Yes, for estates worth less than $7,500.
LOUISIANA	
Set by the court.	Yes, for estates worth less than $50,000.
MAINE	
Must notify known creditors of appointment and must see that a notice is published once a week, for two straight weeks, in a local newspaper.	Yes, for estates worth less than $10,000.
MARYLAND	
Must notify known creditors of appointment and must see that a notice is published once a week, for three straight weeks, in a local newspaper.	Yes, for estates worth less than $20,000.

| NOTICE REQUIREMENTS TO CREDITORS: | ARE THERE SIMPLIFIED RULES FOR SMALL ESTATES? |

MASSACHUSETTS

None required unless estate is insolvent.

Yes, for estates worth less than $15,000.

MICHIGAN

Court has notice published prior to hearing on creditor claims.

Yes, for estates worth less than $5,000.

MINNESOTA

Must notify known creditors of appointment and must see that a notice is published once a week, for two straight weeks, in a local newspaper.

Yes, for estates worth less than $30,000.

MISSISSIPPI

Must notify known creditors of appointment and must see that a notice is published once a week, for three straight weeks, in a local newspaper.

Only for estates worth less than $20,000.

MISSOURI

Must notify known creditors of appointment and must see that a notice is published once a week, for four straight weeks, in a local newspaper.

Yes, for estates worth less than $15,000.

MONTANA

Must notify known creditors of appointment and must see that a notice is published once a week, for three straight weeks, in a local newspaper.

Yes, for estates worth less than $7,500.

NEBRASKA

Must notify known creditors of appointment and, within 30 days of appointment, must see that a notice is published once a week, for three straight weeks, in a local newspaper.

Yes, for estates worth less than $10,000.

NEVADA

Must notify known creditors of appointment and must see that a notice is published once a week, for three straight weeks, in a local newspaper.

Yes, for estates worth less than $100,000.

NOTICE REQUIREMENTS TO CREDITORS:	ARE THERE SIMPLIFIED RULES FOR SMALL ESTATES?

NEW HAMPSHIRE

Must notify known creditors of appointment and, within 15 days of appointment, must see that a notice is published once a week, for two straight weeks, in a local newspaper.

Yes, for estates worth less than $5,000.

NEW JERSEY

Must notify known creditors of appointment and, within 20 days of court order, must see that a notice is published once a week, for two straight weeks, in a local newspaper.

Yes, for estates worth less than $10,000.

NEW MEXICO

Must notify known creditors of appointment and must see that a notice is published once a week, for two straight weeks, in a local newspaper.

Yes, for estates worth less than the sum of $20,000.

NEW YORK

Must notify known creditors of appointment and should, but is not necessarily required to, see that a notice is published once a week, for three straight weeks, in a local newspaper.

Yes, for estates worth less than $10,000.

NORTH CAROLINA

Must notify known creditors of appointment and, within 20 days after appointment, must see that a notice is published once a week, for four straight weeks, in a local newspaper.

Yes, for estates worth less than $10,000.

NORTH DAKOTA

Must notify known creditors of appointment and must see that a notice is published once a week, for three straight weeks, in a local newspaper.

Yes, for estates worth less than $15,000.

OHIO

Must notify known creditors of appointment and must see that a notice is published once a week, for three straight weeks, in a local newspaper.

Yes, for estates worth less than $25,000.

NOTICE REQUIREMENTS TO CREDITORS:	ARE THERE SIMPLIFIED RULES FOR SMALL ESTATES?
OKLAHOMA	
Must notify known creditors of appointment and must see that a notice is published once a week, for two straight weeks, in a local newspaper.	Yes, for estates worth less than $60,000.
OREGON	
Must notify known creditors of appointment and must see that a notice is published once a week, for three straight weeks, in a local newspaper.	Yes, for estates worth less than $60,000.
PENNSYLVANIA	
Must notify known creditors of appointment and, as soon as possible after appointment, must see that a notice is published once a week, for three straight weeks, in a local newspaper and in a local legal periodical.	Yes, for estates worth less than $10,000 in personal property.
RHODE ISLAND	
Must notify known creditors of appointment. Court will determine any additional requirements such as publishing notice of appointment.	Yes, for estates worth less than $7,500.
SOUTH CAROLINA	
Must notify known creditors of appointment and, as soon as possible after appointment, must see that a notice is published once a week, for three straight weeks, in a local newspaper.	Yes, for estates worth less than $10,000.
SOUTH DAKOTA	
Must notify known creditors of appointment and must see that a notice is published once a week, for three straight weeks, in a local newspaper.	Yes, for estates worth less than $60,000.

NOTICE REQUIREMENTS TO CREDITORS:	ARE THERE SIMPLIFIED RULES FOR SMALL ESTATES?

TENNESSEE

Must notify known creditors of appointment and, within 30 days after appointment, must see that a notice is published once a week, for two straight weeks, in a local newspaper.

Yes, for estates worth less than $10,000.

TEXAS

Must notify known creditors of appointment and must see that a notice is published in a local newspaper.

Yes, for estates worth less than $50,000.

UTAH

Must notify known creditors of appointment and must see that a notice is published once a week, for three straight weeks, in a local newspaper.

Yes, for estates worth less than $25,000.

VERMONT

Must notify known creditors of appointment and, within 30 days of appointment, must see that a notice is published once a week, for two straight weeks, in a local newspaper.

Yes, for estates worth less than $10,000 in personal property and with no real estate.

VIRGIN ISLANDS

Must notify known creditors of appointment and, as soon as possible after appointment, must see that a notice is published once a week, for four straight weeks, in a local newspaper. The court will also have the notice of appointment published in two "public places" and a post office.

Yes, for estates worth less than $300.

VIRGINIA

Must notify known creditors of appointment and must see that a notice is published once a week, for four straight weeks, in a local newspaper.

Yes, for estates worth less than $5,000.

WASHINGTON

Must notify known creditors of appointment and must see that a notice is published once a week, for three straight weeks, in a local newspaper.

Yes, for estates worth less than $30,000.

NOTICE REQUIREMENTS TO CREDITORS:	ARE THERE SIMPLIFIED RULES FOR SMALL ESTATES?

WEST VIRGINIA

Must notify known creditors of appointment and must see that a notice is published once a week, for two straight weeks, in a local newspaper.

Yes, for estates worth less than $50,000.

WISCONSIN

Must notify known creditors of appointment and, within 15 days of court order, must see that a notice is published once a week, for three straight weeks, in a local newspaper.

Yes, for estates worth less than $30,000.

WYOMING

Must notify known creditors of appointment and must see that a notice is published once a week, for three straight weeks, in a local newspaper.

Yes, for estates worth less than $70,000.

Chapter
4

INVENTORYING THE ESTATE

Now that you've opened the estate and sent out the notices to creditors required by law, you're ready to begin your next important duty as executor: inventorying the estate. You are required to report all of the assets in the estate to the court within a couple of months after opening the estate. Check this chapter's appendix for your state's deadline. Usually, the state requires you to file the inventory within three or four months after opening the estate, although some state deadlines are as short as 30 days and some are as long as six months or more. Ask the local courthouse's clerk's office to send you any standard forms that you are required to file in connection with the inventory. A model inventory form is included at the end of this chapter.

Here is a list of the six basic steps to take in inventorying the estate:

Step 1: Open an Estate Bank Account.

As the executor, you have a fiduciary duty (as defined in the Glossary) to the estate, which requires you to keep all estate funds in a safe place. This means that you must open a bank account, not only for depositing estate funds but also for paying estate expenses. Therefore, opening the estate bank account is important not only for the estate inventory, but for your other executor duties that will be discussed in Chapters 5, 6, and 7.

You should open the estate bank account in a bank with branches in the city or county where the estate was opened. Be sure that the bank is FDIC-insured. Because FDIC deposit insurance only goes up to $100,000 per bank account, however, if the estate is worth more than $100,000, make sure that the bank has a solid reputation and isn't in financial trouble, as so many banks are these days. If you're unsure about which banks are safe and which aren't, the reference section of your public library should have information. Several companies publish guides to banks' financial security. Moody's and Standard and Poor's are the two best guides. Moody's highest rating is Aaa and S&P's is AAA. If a bank has either an Aaa or an AAA rating, you can open the estate bank account there with confidence in the bank's stability.

When you contact banks, be sure to ask specifically about opening an estate account. Estate accounts are common, so the bank should know what you are talking about. You should check with several banks, in the same way that you would check with several banks about opening an ordinary checking account. Does the bank pay interest on estate accounts? It should. Does the bank charge a fee for each check you write on the estate account? Watch out if it does: check fees can add up. The bank should also be able to provide you with preprinted checks for the estate account.

Each check should say "estate account of (name of deceased)," or words to that effect. Such checks make it clear to third parties who receive them that you are acting on behalf of the estate. Remember the discussion on your potential liability as an executor in Chapter 1. Appendix One referred to your potential liability "for estate contracts if the executor fails to reveal that he or she is acting on behalf of the estate." If someone gets an estate check, it's very hard to argue that you didn't reveal you were acting on behalf of an estate.

Finally, the bank should also provide you with an "estate ledger," which is basically a large checkbook in which you should record all estate debits (checks written) and estate credits (deposits). You are responsible for maintaining an accurate estate ledger, so keep it in a safe place.

Step 2: Transfer the Deceased's Cash Assets Into the Estate Account.

You need to close out all of the deceased's checking accounts, savings accounts, and other bank accounts by transferring them to the estate account. Contact the bank or banks where the deceased's accounts are located and ask about the easiest means of accomplishing this. They may ask for a copy of your Letters, but there should be no problem getting the accounts transferred.

You should also transfer any Certificates of Deposit (CD) into the estate account. If there is a substantial penalty for early withdrawal, or the CD pays significantly more interest, you should be able to let the CD sit until it matures. However, check with the local courthouse's clerk's office first. Further, there is the question of how you should handle stock certificates and bonds. If there is a will and the will specifically states that the deceased's stocks and/or bonds are to be given to someone (this is called a "specific bequest"), then you cannot sell them. Otherwise, you will probably be required to sell the deceased's stocks and bonds, and transfer the proceeds into the estate account.

First, review the relevant state principles concerning joint-property ownership of personal property as summarized in Appendix Two. Stocks and bonds are both personal property, as are other financial instruments such as CDs, savings bonds, options, warrants, and promissory notes. If the deceased's state permits personal property to be held as joint property, see if any of the certificates refer to another person's joint-property interest. It may be that they aren't part of the estate after all, but go automatically to someone else.

Before selling any of the deceased's stocks or bonds, however, call the clerk's office and ask the following three questions: (1) Should I sell the stocks or bonds before or after I file the inventory and appraisal? (Appraisals are discussed later in this chapter). (2) Do 1 need court approval before paying a broker's commission out of the estate account? (3) If the stocks or bonds go up in value after I sell them, will I face any sort of personal liability? The answer to question 1 will depend on local practice, and the answers to questions 2 and 3 will usually be no. But you should always check with the clerk's office as to the proper procedure. After selling any stocks or bonds, put the proceeds in the estate accounts.

Step 3: Collect All Income Due to the Deceased.

You need to make a diligent search for any money that might be owed to the deceased so you can collect it and put it in the estate account. As the executor, you have the right to demand payment. If someone owes the deceased money but won't pay, check with the clerk's office about what you should do. You might have to hire a lawyer to sue. Ask the clerk's office if legal fees for collecting estate debts can be paid by you out of the estate account. The answer will usually be yes, but always check first. Here is a list of different types of income that might be owed to the deceased's estate.

1. Wages. Check with the deceased's employer and the deceased's surviving spouse concerning whether there might be any paychecks due to the deceased.

2. Employee Benefits. In addition to wages, various employee benefits may be due to the deceased that you can collect. For example, accrued vacation time, accrued sick leave, retirement plans such as IRAs or 401(k)s (including any employer matching funds), employee profit-sharing plans, employee stock-ownership plans, unpaid bonuses, unpaid overtime, unpaid commissions, unpaid employee-expense reimbursements (such as for travel, meals, or lodging while on company business), and so forth.

3. Debts. If someone owed money to the deceased, you must collect it. Collectible debts include money borrowed by the deceased's business partners, friends, and even relatives. Because of your fiduciary duty to the estate, you may have to be hard-nosed if the deceased's friends or relatives won't pay up. If they owe a lot of money, don't be afraid to say you'll sue if you have to.

4. Government Entitlements. Because most people these days don't die until they are well into their seventies, eighties, or even nineties, the deceased may have been receiving payments under a number of government programs. For example, the deceased might have been collecting federal Social Security, veterans' administration, Medicare, Medicaid, Railroad Retirement Fund, or farm-subsidy benefits. In addition, there may have been state government benefits. Check the deceased's records to see if any payments are due but have not yet been paid. If so, you must contact the appropriate federal or state agency and demand payment. Do *not* assume that they will pay any overdue amounts simply because the deceased's spouse has applied for any eligible death benefits. One hand of the bureaucracy doesn't always know what the other hand is doing, and it's up to you to prod the system into action with your phone calls and letters if payment isn't prompt.

5. Insurance. Most insurance policies name a beneficiary, such as a spouse. If the deceased had life insurance naming a beneficiary such as his or her spouse, then the proceeds of the policy pass to the beneficiary automatically and you don't need to worry about it since it passes outside of the estate. Sometimes, however, people have fire, accident, casualty, or automobile insurance policies in which they were entitled to collect as the result of some incident but never got around to doing so before they died. If this is the case with the deceased, you must collect from the insurance company. Again, don't assume the insurance company will pay of its own volition: usually you have to be persistent with them.

6. Testamentary Interests. If the deceased had any inheritance coming to him or her before he or she died, it's your responsibility to collect it.

7. Miscellaneous. There are all sorts of other types of income, for example: (a) royalties, (b) dividends, (c) interest, (d) alimony, (e) rent or other income due on investment property, (f) federal and state tax refunds, and (g) unemployment compensation. If, in your review of the deceased's records, you discover any money due to the deceased from these or other sources, it is your duty to contact the person or company that owes it. Once you contact them, explain that you are the executor and demand payment of the amount due.

Step 4: Determine If Assets Exist in Other States.

Check the Legal Audit and your search for income due to the estate under Step 3. Are there any assets of the estate, or monies due to the estate, located in other states'? If there are, particularly real estate, you may need to get an "Ancillary Representative" or "'Co-Personal Representative" in the other state or states to collect the debt or administer the real estate. Check with the courthouse of the city or county where the person or company indebted to the deceased resides or where the real estate is located about what is required.

In order to give you the necessary legal authority, a good will, like the form included with Chapter 1, will have a clause resembling the following:

> If for any reason it is necessary at any time for the property adminis- tration of my estate that there by a Personal Representative who is a resident of a particular jurisdiction in which property forming a part of my estate is situated (whether within or without the United States), and if at such time there is no Personal Representative hereof who is a resident of such jurisdiction, then I authorize my Personal Repre- sentative to appoint a special or ancillary Co-Personal Representa- tive who is an individual resident of (or a bank, trust company or similar corporate institution qualified to act in) such other jurisdiction, with unlimited power in my Personal Representative to remove, and to appoint substitutes and successors for, such special and ancillary Co- Personal Representative when the need therefore arises. Said special or ancillary Co-Personal Representative so appointed shall have the power to act only with respect to those matters which necessitated his, her or its appointment, and shall have no authority to participate in any decision by my Personal Representative as to property not lo- cated in the jurisdiction of his, her or its residence, or as to distribu- tion of income or principal.

This clause is Article Ninth, section (B), of the Chapter 1 form, but can be located anywhere in a will and still be legally valid. If the deceased's will has no such clause, or there is no will, check with the deceased's local courthouse's clerk's office to see if any special requirements are imposed by the deceased's state (over and above those of the state where the prop- erty is located) concerning out-of-state executors. There shouldn't be, but you must check just in case. Note the reference in the sample to a "bank, trust company or similar corporate institution": if you can't find a relative of the deceased or other person to be Ancillary Executor, you may have to hire one of these in the area to do the job. Again, check with the deceased's local courthouse's clerk's office concerning any possible limitation on the fee that you can pay such a corporate Ancillary Executor for their services— you want to be sure that the estate can pay for it.

Step 5: Appraisals.

An appraisal means an informed, good-faith assessment of the value of a piece of property. Normally, all of the property in the estate must be appraised. As set forth in this chapter's appendix, the appraisal deadline is usually identical to the inventory deadline. When property value is easy to determine, the state may let the executor appraise it. For example, take the debts to decedent, stocks and bonds, and bank accounts and cash catego- ries of the inventory form set forth on page 96. If there are $5,000 in debts owed, $10,000 in stocks and bonds, and $15,000 in bank accounts and cash, then the value of each item is straightforward: $5,000, $10,000, and $15,000. No special appraising ability is necessary. Check with the local courthouse's clerk's office about whether you can appraise the value of inventory items whose dollar value is obvious and straightforward.

> *Example:* Bill and Hillary live in state X, which permits executors to value securities on their own. After accidentally inhaling something bad for his metabolism, Bill died, leaving Hillary as his executor. Bill's estate includes 10,000 shares of Chicken Feathers, Inc. Hillary looks in the business section of the local paper and sees that Chicken Feathers' stock is quoted at $10 a share. What can Hillary appraise the stock for?

> *Answer:* Ten thousand shares multiplied by $10 equals $100,000, so Hillary can, in good faith, say that the value of the Chicken Feathers stock is $100,000.

In order to do the appraisals for other types of estate property, you will need to (1) hire a professional appraiser with estate funds, or (2) get a court-appointed appraiser. For example, you will probably need an appraiser to value real estate such as investment property and vacation homes. In addition to real estate, you may have to get an appraiser to value personal property such as works of art and jewelry. If you have to get an appraiser, be sure to ask (1) whether you need a professional appraiser or a court-appointed appraiser, (2) if you need a professional appraiser, does he or she have to be certified by any particular state agency or private organization, (3) if you need a court-appointed appraiser, what do you have to do to get one, and (4) do you need different appraisers for different types of property, such as real estate versus expensive personal property.

When the appraiser tells you what the property is worth, you use that dollar figure in filling out the inventory form. The appraiser should give you his or her estimate of the property's value in writing. Save these written appraisals because you may have to file them with the court when you file the inventory.

Real-Estate Appraisals. Because real-estate appraisals are the most common and frequently the most expensive type of appraisal, I will give a short overview of what's involved. Real estate that people live in, such as houses, townhouses, condominiums, and cooperatives, are the easiest to appraise. The appraiser goes to the property, checks its overall condition, looks at what comparable homes in the neighborhood have sold for recently, and then makes his or her estimate. An appraisal of a residential property shouldn't cost the estate more than a couple hundred dollars. If the residential property takes more research to estimate its value, such as for a mansion or a farm, then the appraisal will cost more.

In addition to residential real estate, the deceased may have had some commercial real-estate interest. For example, if the deceased was a businessman or an investor, he may have had an ownership interest in a store or a partnership interest in an office. Such commercial properties are harder to appraise. The appraiser can't rely so much on what comparable business properties in the area have sold for recently because business properties don't sell as often as residential real estate. Therefore, in making their value estimates appraisers look at (1) what it would cost to build an identical commercial property from scratch and (2) what kind of income, such as rents or gross business sales, come from the property. This takes more time, and such an appraisal is more expensive, often costing several thousand dollars.

Personal-Property Appraisals. Usually, only valuable personal property such as works of art and jewelry must be included in the inventory. For example, many states say you don't have to include the deceased's clothing in the inventory (unless there's something with value on the open market, like furs). If clothes or any other type of personal property don't have to be on the inventory, they obviously don't have to be appraised.

Step 6: Prepare and File the Estate Inventory.

After having completed Steps 1 through 5, you should have the information necessary to complete the inventory forms, comply with the appraisal requirements, and file everything with the court. Although the forms may be short, like the sample below, check with the clerk's office about whether you have to submit any additional documentation. For example, you may be required to submit written appraisals for certain types of estate property, as discussed in Step 5.

If you filed an incomplete inventory, or made a mistake in completing the forms, the clerk's office will probably call or write you and give you some time to correct the error by filing proper forms if the error isn't serious. If the error is serious, you might have to appear in court before a judge to explain what happened. Therefore, *be careful:* being an executor is a serious responsibility, so take the time necessary to fill out the forms completely, thoroughly, and accurately.

(You will probably have to file supporting schedules with additional details, including any relevant appraisals.)

IN THE ORPHANS' COURT FOR
(OR) _____ , MARYLAND
BEFORE THE REGISTER OF WILLS FOR

IN THE ESTATE OF:

_____ ESTATE NO: _____

INVENTORY
Summary

Schedule	Type of Property	Appraised Value
A	Real	$
B	Leasehold	$
C	Tangible personal	$
D	Corporate stocks	$
E	Bonds, notes, mortgages, debts due to the decedent	$
F	Bank accounts, savings and loan accounts, cash	$
G	All other interests	$

Total .... $

I solemnly affirm under the penalties of perjury that the contents of the foregoing inventory are true to the best of my knowledge, information, and belief and that any property valued by me which I have authority as personal representative to appraise has been valued completely and correctly in accordance with law.

| _____ | _____ | _____ |
| Attorney | Personal Representative | Date |

| _____ | _____ | _____ |
| Address | Personal Representative | Date |

| _____ | _____ | _____ |
| | Personal Representative | Date |

_____
Telephone Number

INVENTORY
Supporting Schedule

Inventory of Estate of _____

Estate No _____

SCHEDULE _____

Item No.	Description	Name and Address of Appraiser	Market Value

Total $ _____

APPENDIX FOUR

Fifty-state summary of deadlines for executors to prepare inventories, have estates appraised, and file inventories with local courts. Also includes the District of Columbia and the Virgin Islands. State laws change periodically, so be certain to confirm the information set forth below concerning your state with an authoritative source, such as the court clerk's office or if necessary an attorney.

ALABAMA

Within three months after being appointed.

ALASKA

Within three months after being appointed.

ARIZONA

Within three months after being appointed.

ARKANSAS

Within two months after being appointed.

CALIFORNIA

Within four months after being appointed.

COLORADO

Within three months after being appointed.

CONNECTICUT

Within two months after being appointed.

DELAWARE

Within three months after being appointed.

DISTRICT OF COLUMBIA

Within three months after being appointed.

FLORIDA

Within 60 days after being appointed.

GEORGIA

Within four months after being appointed.

HAWAII

Within 30 days after being appointed.

IDAHO

Within three months after being appointed.

ILLINOIS

Within 60 days after being appointed.

INDIANA

Within two months after being appointed.

IOWA

Within 90 days after being appointed.

KANSAS

Within 30 days after being appointed.

KENTUCKY

Within two months after being appointed.

LOUISIANA

Only if requested by inheritor.

MAINE

Within three months after being appointed.

MARYLAND

Within three months after being appointed.

MASSACHUSETTS

Within three months after being appointed.

MICHIGAN

Within 60 days after being appointed.

MINNESOTA

Within six months after being appointed.

MISSISSIPPI

Within 90 days after being appointed.

MISSOURI

Within 30 days after being appointed.

MONTANA

Usually within three months after being appointed.

NEBRASKA

Within two months after being appointed.

NEVADA

Within 60 days after being appointed.

NEW HAMPSHIRE

Within three months after being appointed.

NEW JERSEY

Not required unless the court orders it.

NEW MEXICO

Within three months after being appointed.

NEW YORK

Within six months after being appointed.

NORTH CAROLINA

Within three months after being appointed.

NORTH DAKOTA

Within six months after being appointed, or nine months after deceased's death, whichever is later.

OHIO

Within one month after being appointed. Special note: In Ohio, the surviving spouse is entitled to one automobile from the estate, and that automobile is not considered an asset of the estate, and is not included on the estate inventory.

OKLAHOMA

Within two months after being appointed.

OREGON

Within 60 days after being appointed.

PENNSYLVANIA

Usually within four months after being appointed.

RHODE ISLAND

Within 30 days after being appointed.

SOUTH CAROLINA

Within 60 days after being appointed.

SOUTH DAKOTA

Within nine months after the date of deceased's death.

TENNESSEE

Within 60 days after being appointed.

TEXAS

Within 90 days after being appointed.

UTAH

Within three months after being appointed.

VERMONT

Within 30 days after being appointed.

VIRGIN ISLANDS

Within 30 days after being appointed.

VIRGINIA

Within four months after being appointed.

WASHINGTON

Within three months after being appointed.

WEST VIRGINIA

Within 14 months after being appointed.

WISCONSIN

Within six months after being appointed.

WYOMING

Within 120 days after being appointed.

HANDLING CLAIMS AGAINST THE ESTATE AND ESTATE TAXES

Now that you've filed the estate inventory and taken care of all the appraisal obligations, you can proceed to the next tasks: (1) paying off claims against the estate and (2) paying those special federal and state taxes levied against estates and thus known generically as "estate taxes."

1. Paying Off Claims Against the Estate.

In Chapter 3, I discussed your legal duty to notify all of the deceased's creditors. Assuming that you have notified all such creditors, you can turn to this chapter's appendix to find out when the creditor has to file his, her, or its claim. For example, the state may require that creditors file their claims within three months after you, the executor, were appointed. If creditors don't file their claims on time, they don't become legal "claimants." Generally, you are required to pay only claimants. Of course, you don't have to pay claimants if you think that their claim is unjustified or inflated— you don't have to pay them simply because they've filed a claim. Call the clerk's office of the local courthouse concerning denying claims and what procedures you must follow.

Assuming that, by the end of the creditors' deadline, you have received claims that are all valid, you can generally pay them as you see fit at any time before the estate is closed. What happens, however, if the estate doesn't have enough money to pay all the creditors? Not only may the heirs or beneficiaries end up getting nothing from the estate, because usually the estate has to pay off all valid claims first, but you have to be sure that you pay off creditors according to the state priority statutes.

Every state has laws that stipulate which creditors must be paid before other creditors are if the estate cannot pay all creditors. This chapter's appendix lists every state's claims with priority. Let me give you some examples of how priority claims work:

Example: Under the laws of State X, the following claims have priority: (1) administrative expenses, (2) funeral expenses, (3) last illness expenses, and (4) all other creditors. Assume that the estate has $20,000 in assets and the following claims against it: (1) $1,000 in administrative expenses, (2) $9,000 in funeral expenses, (3) $15,000 in last-illness expenses, and (4) $100,000 in credit card bills. Who gets what?

Answer: Because they are number 1, all $1,000 in administrative expenses must be paid. Then, all $9,000 in funeral expenses must be paid, because they are number 2. Last-illness expenses are $15,000, but there's only $10,000 (two thirds of the total amount due) to pay number-3 expenses. If there's only one last-illness creditor, they get the $10,000 but nothing more; they lose the additional $5,000 because there's nothing left. If there's more than one last-illness creditor, each creditor gets a *prorated* share: there's only enough money to pay two-thirds of last-illness expenses, so each creditor gets only two-thirds of their claim and loses the rest. For example, if the $15,000 in last-illness expenses was composed of one claim for $5,000 and another for $10,000, then each gets two-thirds: the $5,000 claimant gets only $3,333 and the $10,000 creditor gets only $6,667.

The credit-card companies are the big losers. Because they are number 4 and the estate's assets ran out in priority number 3, the credit-card companies get *nothing* for their $100,000 in claims. Of course, the deceased's spouse may have been a co-signer on the credit-card agreements, but if the credit-card companies try to collect from the spouse that won't affect the estate.

Insolvent Estates. When an estate doesn't have enough money to pay all claims, such as in the question above, it is called an "insolvent estate." An insolvent estate isn't always bad: it may mean that the deceased did such a good job of estate planning that most property passed outside of the estate and the creditors are left holding the bag because few assets are left in the estate. This is perfectly legal to do, because creditors could always have demanded payment while the deceased was alive or gotten more security (such as additional co-signers in the credit-card example above). Further, if the estate is insolvent, there is no threat to property passing outside of the estate such as tenancy-by-the-entirety property, joint-tenancy property, or life-insurance proceeds to the policy's beneficiaries.

Types of Priority Creditors. As you may have guessed, most state claims priorities aren't as simple as those of the hypothetical State X. Further, you need to know more about what constitutes an "administrative expense" and other such creditor designations. Here are most of the different types of creditors that may or may not be given priority in your state. If they are given priority, they may not be given priority in the order set forth below. Therefore, you should always (1) check this chapter's appendix and (2) call the local courthouse's clerk's office to see if they have any additional guidance for you.

(i) *Administrative expenses.* This refers to the expenses involved in opening, running, and closing the estate. These expenses are usually the first priority. They may include (1) court filing fees, (2) professional appraisers' fees, (3) attorneys' fees, if you have to hire an attorney to help you in legal matters respecting the estate, and (4) the cost of obtaining your executor's bond from an insurance company. Further, administrative expenses usually include (5) the fees that you are entitled to collect from the estate for your services as executor (see Chapter 7 and its appendix), and (6) accountants' fees, if you hire CPAs to help you with estate tax and accounting duties. Because you can thus usually pay accountants' fees as a number-one priority item, later in this Chapter I strongly recommend that you hire an accountant to take care of the estate's taxes rather than try to handle them on your own.

(ii) *Funeral expenses.* This refers to all of the various funeral and burial expenses, such as (1) funeral-home charges, (2) purchase price of a plot, and (3) embalming or cremation expenses. Sometimes, however, there is a limit on what can be spent for funeral expenses. If this limit is exceeded, the excess may be treated as a lower priority claim.

(iii) *Allowance to surviving spouse and children.* Often referred to as the family allowance, this refers to a certain dollar amount that state law may set up as a *priority creditor* so that the deceased's spouse and/or children will always receive something, even if the estate is insolvent. Sometimes the family allowance is related to the automatic share spouses are entitled to under state law, but in any event the state will probably specify a certain dollar amount if it has a family allowance.

(iv) *Debts (and taxes) with preference under federal law.* Simply put, this means monies the deceased owed to the federal government. *Debts* may refer to such things as criminal fines against the deceased or unpaid federal obligations such as student loans. "Taxes" refers to the deceased's unpaid federal tax obligations, such as personal income tax, gift tax, quarterly estimated tax, and so forth.

Keep in mind that unlike other creditors, the IRS usually doesn't have to file a notice of claim. There are two reasons for this. First, as discussed later in this chapter, you the executor are responsible for getting the deceased's federal tax returns filed for the year of death. Second, for taxes the deceased owed from previous years, there may be IRS *tax liens* on record against the deceased. Call the deceased's accountant and ask whether there are any IRS tax liens against the deceased. If the deceased didn't have an accountant, and you suspect that he or she was behind in his or her federal taxes, check the federal government telephone listings or call directory assistance for the number of the IRS district office nearest the deceased's residence. Then, call that office, explain that you are the deceased's executor, and ask for information concerning tax liens.

Finally, don't confuse federal taxes in this creditor-priority category with the federal estate tax, discussed below. The federal estate tax is imposed only after people die, and does not concern the taxes discussed in this category.

(v) *Last-illness expenses.* Most states give the deceased's debts relating to his or her last illness or hospital treatment before death a high priority status. This is designed to encourage medical providers to give all necessary treatments without fear that they will be unpaid if the patient dies. Last-illness expenses may include the deceased's debts for (1) hospital treatment, (2) doctors' and nurses' care, (3) outpatient or home-health care, (4) physical and rehabilitation therapy, (5) drug and alcohol detoxification, (6) prescription drugs, and (7) medical paraphernalia such as wheelchairs and crutches.

(vi) *Taxes due.* Sometimes the federal taxes discussed in (iv) above and the state taxes discussed in (vii) below are given a separate creditor-priority category which applies to taxes only.

(vii) *Debts (and taxes) with preference under state law.* This is related to creditor-preference category (iv) above. Sometimes the state lumps this category (vii) together with (iv) to create a joint federal-state debt and tax category. Other times, the state gives state debts and taxes a different priority. Further, the state may not give priority to debts and taxes due to *other* states: for example, in this chapter's appendix you'll see that in Colorado the preference is only for "debts and taxes with preference under *Colorado* law." In addition to the appendix, however, always check with the local courthouse's clerk's office if the estate has debts and/or taxes due to other states: there may be local procedures or interpretations of the law concerning paying out-of-state claims.

Debts may include not only debts to the state or state agencies, but debts to arms of the state government like local city and county municipal authorities. Therefore, the trash removal or water bill from the deceased's municipal government may be entitled to a "debts" preference. *Taxes* refers to the deceased's unpaid state and possibly local tax obligations, such as personal income tax, property tax, and if the deceased was a businessman, perhaps business-related taxes such as sales taxes.

Like the IRS, state and local tax authorities may not have to file a notice of claim. Again, there are two reasons for this. First, as with federal taxes, you are responsible for getting the deceased's state and local tax returns filed for the year of death. Second, for taxes the deceased owed from previous years, there may be state and local tax liens on record against the deceased. If you call the deceased's accountant about IRS tax liens, therefore, also ask about state and local tax liens against the deceased. If the deceased didn't have an accountant, and you suspect that he or she was behind in his or her state or local taxes, then check the state and local government telephone listings or call directory assistance for the numbers of the state and local agencies that collect taxes. Check with these agencies for information concerning tax liens. If there are no federal tax liens, don't assume that means there are no state or local tax liens. It is possible that the deceased paid all his or her federal taxes, but not all state or local taxes.

Finally, as with federal taxes, don't confuse state and local taxes in this creditor-priority category with any state estate tax, credit estate tax, or inheritance tax discussed below. These state taxes are imposed only after people die, and do not concern the taxes discussed in this category.

(viii) *Wages.* The deceased may have had servants, such as a live-in nurse or maid if the deceased was very old or sick. Further, if the deceased had a business that he or she was running as a sole proprietorship, the deceased may have had some employees who worked for him or her personally and not for a business entity. State law may give the deceased's servants and employees some priority-creditor status for unpaid wages. For example, you'll see in this chapter's appendix that Connecticut gives a priority for "wages due to the deceased's employees within three months of the date of death." If there are wages due for more than three months in Connecticut, or for whatever period is relevant in other states, the excess isn't lost but gets a lesser priority status, such as "other debts."

(ix) *Mortgages and other liens not already secured.* This is a creditor-preference category that involves the concept of *secured creditors.* Let me explain.

Some types of loans are secured by collateral. For example, a home mortgage is secured by the house, a car loan is secured by the car, and so forth. If a creditor's debt is secured by collateral, the creditor is a secured creditor. Secured creditors have to be paid off first if the collateral is sold, and state creditor-preference categories are irrelevant.

> *Example:* The deceased owned a vacation home, not as joint property, but in her name only. The house is worth $150,000 and was financed with a $100,000 mortgage. If you the executor have to sell the house in order to pay off estate creditors, the mortgage company must be paid off first. The remaining $50,000 goes into the estate to pay off creditors.

What if the collateral isn't worth enough to pay off the secured creditor? The secured creditor may file a notice of claim against the estate, but because the collateral isn't involved anymore the secured creditor isn't secured. That's what this category (ix) is all about: the creditor may or may not have a priority for its unsecured claim.

Example: The deceased owned a vacation home, not as joint property, but in her name only. Because of a bad real-estate market, the house is worth only $50,000. It was financed with a $100,000 mortgage. If the mortgage company forecloses on the house and sells it for $50,000, the company is still owed $50,000. It may be able to file a category (ix) claim against the estate.

Other types of unsecured mortgages and liens in this category include loans, mechanics liens, and other debts not recorded under state law and therefore not secured.

(x) *Judgments.* If the deceased was ever sued while alive and lost his or her case, there may be a court order, called a *judgment,* that gives the person who won the case the right to collect a certain amount of money from the deceased. Some states give such judgment creditors a certain priority. If the judgment comes from an out-of-state court, however, check with the deceased's local courthouse's clerk's office to see if out-of-state judgments get the same priority as in-state judgments if the state has a priority category for judgments.

(xi) *All other debts.* If there is no priority-creditor category in the state that covers a particular creditor, you can only pay that creditor and any other estate debts if there's enough money to pay all priority creditors.

2. Federal and State Taxes.

Federal and State Tax Returns for the Deceased's Last Year of Life. As mentioned above, you the executor are responsible for seeing to the filing of the deceased's final federal, state, and local income tax and other tax returns. I use the expression "see to the filing of" because you can hire an accountant, or use the deceased's accountant, to take care of these tasks and pay their fees out of the estate. As mentioned above, accountants' fees are usually a first-priority administrative expense under state law. Therefore, I recommend that you take advantage of this and use an accountant to take care of the deceased's final tax returns. Of course, if the deceased's final tax returns are not complicated and you are confident of your ability to complete and file them, by all means do so.

Federal Estate Tax and the Various State Death Taxes. You must also see to the payment of the federal estate tax, and state estate and inheritance taxes. State estate and inheritance taxes are typically referred to generically as "death taxes" because they are triggered when a person dies. For example, the estate has to file a Form 706 with the IRS if the gross value of the estate is over a certain amount ($675,000 as of the date of this book). Form 706, with its various supporting schedules, is 30 pages long. The instructions for Form 706 are roughly 20 pages long and IRS Publication 448, *"Federal Estate and Gift Taxes,"* is roughly 40 pages long. The forms, laws, and regulations are very complex. This means that if you try to complete and file the Form 706 yourself, and make a mistake concerning a deduction or some other matter, the loss could be thousands of dollars or more given the large size of the estate involved when Form 706 has to be filed. Therefore, once again, I recommend that you hire an accountant to take care of these matters for you, with the fees to be paid out of the estate as an administrative fee.

Here is a summary of the relevant federal and state taxes involved:

(i) *Federal Estate Tax.* Up to and including 1997, an IRS Form 706 "U.S. Estate (and Generation-Skipping Transfer) Tax Return" had to be filed with the IRS if the deceased's "gross estate" at the time of death was over $600,000. In other words, gross estates under $600,000 were exempt. However, Congress has acted to increase the exemption to $1,000,000, phased in from 1998 to 2006:

1998:	$625,000
1999:	$650,000
2000 and 2001:	$675,000
2002 and 2003:	$700,000
2004:	$850,000
2005:	$950,000
2006 and beyond:	$1,000,000

Be warned: these exemptions, and the entire federal estate tax system, are currently the subject of much controversy in Congress. There are initiatives to eliminate it entirely. If this happens, the state death tax system, which is linked to the federal system, would have to be significantly revised as well.

Calculating the gross estate involves including some items which are not really part of the estate, such as (1) tenancy-by-the-entirety property, (2) joint-tenancy property, (3) community property in community-property states, and (4) life-insurance proceeds, even if the estate is not the beneficiary. The Form 706 must be filed even if the "net estate," which is what the tax to be paid is ultimately based on, is less than the filing requirement amount set forth in the above table. If the net estate is over the relevant exemption amount, the federal estate tax begins at 18 percent and rises to a maximum of 55 percent. However, there is a credit for state death taxes. For every dollar of state death taxes paid (subject to certain maximum limits set forth by the Internal Revenue Code), the amount of federal estate tax due is reduced dollar for dollar. This is a deliberate measure designed to give the states part of the federal estate tax revenue. As you will see in the appendix, state death taxes are tied to the federal estate tax's state tax credit. The state taxing authorities have their own forms and filing requirements, however, which must be complied with in addition to filing the Form 706.

(ii) *Federal Gift Tax.* If the deceased gave more than $10,000 in gifts, in the year he or she died, the estate may have to file a Form 709 with the IRS and pay a federal gift tax.

(iii) *Federal Fiduciary Income Tax Return.* If the estate has (1) annual gross income of over $600 or (2) a beneficiary who is a nonresident alien, you must see to the filing of a Form 1041 with the IRS. There may also be a state fiduciary filing requirement with the state taxing authorities.

(iv) *State estate tax.* There may be a state estate tax imposed on the value of the decedent's estate. This tax may be due even if no federal estate tax is due, since some states tax small estates not subject to any federal liability.

(v) *State inheritance tax.* There may be a state inheritance tax imposed on the amounts received by the various heirs and beneficiaries.

(vi) *Miscellaneous Tax Concerns.* In addition to the above six tax concerns, here are some more tax matters that you and the estate accountant should keep in mind.

(a) As mentioned in category (viii) of my discussion of creditor-priority categories, the deceased may have paid wages to personal servants and business employees. Have all federal, state, and local payroll taxes and withholdings been made?

(b) In order to comply with federal and state estate-tax requirements, the estate will probably have to report life-insurance policies (IRS Form 712), get certain information from the heirs and beneficiaries (IRS Form W-9), and get an estate Taxpayer Identification Number (IRS Form SS-4). There may be other forms, federal and state, that have to be filed. To name but two, there are the Notice Concerning Fiduciary Relationship (IRS Form 56) and the Statement of Person Claiming Refund Due a Deceased Taxpayer (IRS Form 1310). Have all of these requirements been met and the forms filed?

Estate-Tax Audits. While the long arm of the tax collector can't follow the deceased into the hereafter, it can come after his or her estate. If it does, you the executor and the accountant will have much to do.

Ordinary tax audits are unpleasant enough, but estate-tax audits can be even worse. Federal estate-tax audits are conducted by IRS attorneys who specialize in examining Form 706 returns. They have special powers to investigate all of the deceased's financial affairs; so in addition to looking at the deceased's books and records, the IRS estate auditor can get at the books and records of business entities or other individuals with whom the deceased had financial dealings.

IRS estate auditors don't audit every Form 706 return—that would be bureaucratically impossible. Instead, they are trained to look for certain unusual or questionable factors in the return. Here are some of the most important factors in a Form 706 return that can cause an audit.

(i) *Incomplete Form 706s.* If it hasn't been properly signed or all of the questions and schedules completed, this could lead to an estate audit.

(ii) *Internal Inconsistencies.* The Form 706's various schedules and documents have to be consistent. For example, if the will refers to certain types of property which the Form 706 doesn't account for, there might be an audit.

(iii) *Unusually Large Claims by Family Members.* If there are unusually large claims against the estate by the deceased's family members, the IRS may get suspicious that there is an attempt to reduce the taxable "net estate" and initiate an audit. There is no hard-and-fast rule for what constitutes "unusually large claims." It depends on the size of the deceased's estate, the nature of the deceased's Form 706 return, and the relationship of the deceased with his or her family members.

In addition to federal estate audits, there is always the possibility of state death-tax audits for one or more of the various types of state death taxes. Whether or not the state will audit the estate depends upon the enforcement policies of each state's tax authorities.

APPENDIX FIVE

Fifty-state summary of priority-claim statutes (the orders in which creditors must be paid), presentation of claim statutes (the deadlines for creditors to present claims), and applicable state taxes. Includes the District of Columbia and the Virgin Islands. State laws change periodically, so be certain to confirm the information set forth below concerning your state with an authoritative source, such as the court clerk's office or if necessary an attorney.

ALABAMA

Claims with priority:
  (1) Funeral expenses, (2) administrative expenses, (3) expenses during last sickness, (4) taxes owed before deceased's death, (5) any debts to deceased's employees from the year of death, and (6) all other debts.

When creditors must present claims:
  Within five months after executor published notice or six months after the executor is appointed, whichever is later.

State taxes:
  Estate tax plus an additional tax based upon federal estate tax's state tax credit.

ALASKA

Claims with priority:
  (1) Administrative expenses, (2) funeral expenses, (3) debts and taxes with preference under federal law, (4) expenses during last sickness, (5) debts and taxes with preference under state law, and (6) all other debts.

When creditors must present claims:
  Within four months after executor published notice, or within three years after the deceased's death if no notice.

State taxes:
  Estate tax plus an additional tax based upon federal estate tax's state tax credit.

ARIZONA

Claims with priority:

(1) Administrative expenses, (2) funeral expenses, (3) debts and taxes with preference under federal law, (4) expenses during last sickness, (5) debts and taxes with preference under state law, and (6) all other debts.

When creditors must present claims:

Within four months after executor published notice, or within three years after the deceased's death if no notice. Arizona courts have held that these limitations do not apply if creditors do not receive actual notice, however.

State taxes:

Estate tax plus an additional tax based upon federal estate tax's state tax credit.

ARKANSAS

Claims with priority:

(1) Administrative expenses, (2) funeral expenses, last-illness expenses, and any wages due to any of deceased's employees, and (3) all other debts.

When creditors must present claims:

Within three months after executor published notice, or within five years after the deceased's death if no notice.

State taxes:

Estate tax plus an additional tax based upon federal estate tax's state tax credit.

CALIFORNIA

Claims with priority:

(1) Administrative expenses, (2) funeral expenses, (3) expenses of last illness, (4) family allowance, (5) wages, (6) mortgages and other liens not already secured, (7) judgments, and (8) all other debts.

When creditors must present claims:

Within four months after executor published notice, or within 30 days after receiving actual notice, whichever is later.

State taxes:

Estate tax plus an additional tax based upon federal estate tax's state tax credit.

COLORADO

Claims with priority:

(1) Those with property held by the deceased as a fiduciary or trustee, (2) administrative costs, (3) funeral expenses, (4) debts and taxes with preference under federal law, (5) last-illness expenses, (6) debts and taxes with preference under Colorado law, and (7) all other debts.

When creditors must present claims:

Within four months after executor published notice, or within one year after the deceased's death if no notice.

State taxes:

Estate tax plus an additional tax based upon federal estate tax's state tax credit.

CONNECTICUT

Claims with priority:

(1) Funeral and administrative expenses, (2) last-illness expenses, (3) taxes due to the United States or the State of Connecticut, (4) wages due to the deceased's employees within three months of the date of death, (5) certain other preferred claims, and (6) all other debts.

When creditors must present claims:

Anywhere from three months to one year after notice was given, depending on what the court orders on a case-by-case basis.

State taxes:

Inheritance tax based on the federal estate tax's state tax credit.

DELAWARE

Claims with priority:

(1) Administrative expenses, (2) funeral expenses, (3) last-sickness expenses, (4) wages due to deceased's employees for one year prior to death, (5) state taxes, (6) rent due for one year prior to death, (7) various contracts and obligations for payment of money, delivery of goods and so forth, and (8) all other debts.

When creditors must present claims:

Within eight months after date of death, whether or not notice was given.

State taxes:

Inheritance tax based on the federal estate tax's state tax credit.

DISTRICT OF COLUMBIA

Claims with priority:

(1) Family allowance of up to $10,000, (2) back rent, (3) District of Columbia judgments, and (4) all other debts.

When creditors must present claims:

Within six months after executor first published notice.

State taxes:

Estate tax plus an additional tax based upon federal estate tax's state tax credit.

FLORIDA

Claims with priority:

(1) Administrative expenses, (2) $3,000 in funeral expenses, (3) debts and taxes with preference under federal law, (4) last-illness expenses for the 60 days preceding death, (5) family allowance, (6) debts after death due to continuation of the deceased's business to the extent of the business's assets, and (7) all other debts.

When creditors must present claims:

Within three months after executor first published notice.

State taxes:

Estate tax plus an additional tax based upon federal estate tax's state tax credit.

GEORGIA

Claims with priority:
(1) One-year's support for deceased's family, (2) funeral expenses, (3) administrative expenses, (4) taxes or other debts due to the United States or Georgia, (5) debts due by deceased from having been a trustee or other type of fiduciary, (6) judgments, mortgages, and liens against items of specific property, (7) debts for rent, (8) general judgments against the deceased, (9) open accounts, and (10) all other debts.

When creditors must present claims:
Within three months after the executor last published notice.

State taxes:
Estate tax plus an additional tax based upon federal estate tax's state tax credit.

HAWAII

Claims with priority:
(1) Administrative expenses, (2) funeral expenses, (3) up to $6,000 in family allowance, (4) homestead allowance, (5) exempt property, (6) debts and taxes with preference under federal law, (7) last-illness expenses, (8) debts and taxes with preference under Hawaii law, and (9) all other debts.

When creditors must present claims:
Within four months after executor first published notice, or within three years after the deceased's death if no notice.

State taxes:
Estate tax plus an additional tax based upon federal estate tax's state tax credit.

IDAHO

Claims with priority:
(1) Administrative expenses, (2) funeral expenses and last-illness expenses, (3) debts and taxes with preference under federal law or Idaho law, and (4) all other debts.

When creditors must present claims:
Within four months after executor published notice or within three years after the deceased's death if no notice.

State taxes:
Estate tax plus an additional tax based upon federal estate tax's state tax credit.

ILLINOIS

Claims with priority:
(1) Funeral expenses and administrative expenses, (2) surviving spouse's or children's award, (3) debts due to the U.S. government, (4) last-illness expenses and any wages due to the deceased's employees from four months prior to death but no more than $800 per employee, (5) money and property held in trust by the deceased which cannot be traced, (6) debts due to the State of Illinois or any political subdivision, and (7) all other debts.

When creditors must present claims:
Within six months after executor published notice, or within two years after the deceased's death if no notice.

State taxes:

Estate tax plus an additional tax based upon federal estate tax's state tax credit.

INDIANA

Claims with priority:

(1) Administrative expenses, (2) funeral expenses, (3) allowances to spouses or children, (4) debts and taxes with preference under federal law, (5) last-sickness expenses, (6) debts and taxes with preference under Indiana law, and (7) all other debts.

When creditors must present claims:

Within five months after executor first published notice.

State taxes:

Inheritance tax based on the federal estate tax's state tax credit.

IOWA

Claims with priority:

(1) Court costs, (2) other administrative expenses, (3) funeral expenses, (4) debts and taxes with preference under federal law, (5) last-illness expenses, (6) debts and taxes with preference under Iowa law, (7) debts to any of deceased's employees for services within 90 days of death, and (8) all other debts.

When creditors must present claims:

Within four months after executor published notice.

State taxes:

Inheritance tax based on the federal estate tax's state tax credit.

KANSAS

Claims with priority:

(1) Funeral expenses, (2) last-sickness expenses and administrative costs, (3) judgments against deceased rendered during deceased's lifetime, and (4) all other debts.

When creditors must present claims:

Within four months after executor first published notice, or within six months of death if no administration required.

State taxes:

Inheritance tax based on the federal estate tax's state tax credit.

KENTUCKY

Claims with priority:

(1) Administrative expenses, (2) funeral expenses, (3) debts and taxes with preference under federal and Kentucky law, and (4) all other debts.

When creditors must present claims:

Within six months after executor is appointed, or within two years after the date of death if no one is appointed.

State taxes:

Inheritance tax based on the federal estate tax's state tax credit.

LOUISIANA

Claims with priority:

(1) Funeral expenses, (2) charges imposed by law, (3) last-illness expenses, (4) servants' wages for the last year and the current year, (5) amounts due to retailers for family provisions for six months prior to death and rent due to innkeepers or boarding houses for one year prior to death, (6) clerks' salaries, if any, and (7) all other debts.

When creditors must present claims:

Check with local court as to local practice, because Louisiana's unique French civil-law system can allow creditors to present claims for up to five years.

State taxes:

Inheritance tax based on the federal estate tax's state tax credit.

MAINE

Claims with priority:

(1) Administrative expenses, (2) funeral expenses, (3) debts and taxes with preference under federal law, (4) expenses during last sickness, (5) debts and taxes with preference under Maine law, and (6) all other debts.

When creditors must present claims:

Within four months after executor first published notice. If creditor received actual notice, then within 60 days after receipt of notice.

State taxes:

Inheritance tax based on the federal estate tax's state tax credit.

MARYLAND

Claims with priority:

(1) Fees due to the registrar of wills, (2) administrative expenses, (3) funeral expenses, not to exceed $2,500, (4) executor's, real-estate agent's, and attorney's fees, (5) family allowance, (6) taxes due by the deceased, (7) last-illness expenses, (8) up to three months back rent owed by deceased, (9) wages, salaries, and commissions due for services performed for three months prior to death, (10) any Maryland old-age assistance claims, and (11) all other debts.

When creditors must present claims:

Within two months after executor gave notice or six months after the executor is appointed.

State taxes:

Inheritance tax based on the federal estate tax's state tax credit.

MASSACHUSETTS

Claims with priority:

(1) Last-illness expenses, funeral expenses, and administrative expenses, (2) debts with preference under federal law, (3) public rates, taxes, and excise duties, and (4) miscellaneous other small claims and all other debts.

When creditors must present claims:

Within four months after executor posts required bond with court.

State taxes:

Estate tax plus an additional tax based upon federal estate tax's state tax credit.

MICHIGAN

Claims with priority:
(1) Administrative expenses, (2) funeral expenses, (3) family allowances and homestead exemptions, (4) certain claims against the estate such as last-illness expenses and debts due to the federal government or the State of Michigan, and (5) all other debts.

When creditors must present claims:
Within four months after executor first published notice, or within three years after the deceased's death if no notice.

State taxes:
Estate tax plus an additional tax based upon federal estate tax's state tax credit.

MINNESOTA

Claims with priority:
(1) Administrative expenses, (2) funeral expenses, (3) debts and taxes with preference under federal law, (4) last-illness expenses, (5) medical expenses from up to one year preceding deceased's death, (6) debts and taxes with preference under Minnesota law, and (7) all other debts.

When creditors must present claims:
Within three months after executor first published notice.

State taxes:
Estate tax plus an additional tax based upon federal estate tax's state tax credit.

MISSISSIPPI

Claims with priority:
(1) Last-illness expenses, funeral expenses, and administrative expenses, and (2) all other debts.

When creditors must present claims:
Within three months after executor first published notice.

State taxes:
Estate tax plus an additional tax based upon federal estate tax's state tax credit.

MISSOURI

Claims with priority:
(1) Court costs and fees, (2) administrative expenses, (3) exemptions and allowances, (4) funeral expenses, (5) debts and taxes with preference under federal law, (6) last-illness expenses and servants' wages, (7) debts and taxes with preference under Missouri law, (8) judgments rendered against the deceased during his or her lifetime, and (9) all other debts.

When creditors must present claims:
Within three months after executor first published notice, or within three years after the deceased's death if no notice.

State taxes:
Estate tax plus an additional tax based upon federal estate tax's state tax credit.

MONTANA

Claims with priority:
(1) Administrative expenses, (2) funeral expenses and last-illness expenses, (3) U.S. estate taxes and Montana estate and inheritance taxes, (4) debts with preference under federal and Montana law, (5) any other federal taxes or Montana taxes, and (6) all other debts.

When creditors must present claims:
Within four months after executor published notice or within three years after the deceased's death if no notice.

State taxes:
Inheritance tax based on the federal estate tax's state tax credit.

NEBRASKA

Claims with priority:
(1) Administrative expenses, (2) funeral expenses, (3) debts and taxes with preference under federal law, (4) last-illness expenses, (5) debts and taxes with preference under Nebraska law, and (6) all other debts.

When creditors must present claims:
Within two months after executor published notice, or within three years after the deceased's death if no notice.

State taxes:
Inheritance tax based on the federal estate tax's state tax credit.

NEVADA

Claims with priority:
(1) Funeral expenses, (2) last-illness expenses, (3) family allowance, (4) debts with preference under federal law, (5) up to $600 in wages for services to the deceased in the 120 days prior to death, (6) judgments and liens against the deceased, and (7) all other debts.

When creditors must present claims:
Within 90 days after executor first published notice.

State taxes:
Estate tax plus an additional tax based upon federal estate tax's state tax credit.

NEW HAMPSHIRE

Claims with priority:
(1) Administrative expenses, (2) funeral expenses, (3) widow's allowance, (4) unpaid taxes, (5) last-illness expenses, and (6) all other debts.

When creditors must present claims:
Within six months after executor was appointed.

State taxes:
Inheritance tax based on the federal estate tax's state tax credit.

New Jersey

Claims with priority:

(1) Funeral expenses, (2) administrative expenses, (3) debts and taxes with preference under federal or New Jersey law, (4) last-illness expenses, (5) judgments against the deceased, and (6) all other debts.

When creditors must present claims:

Within three months after executor first published notice.

State taxes:

Inheritance tax based on the federal estate tax's state tax credit.

New Mexico

Claims with priority:

(1) Administrative expenses, (2) last-illness expenses, (3) funeral expenses, (4) debts and taxes with preference under federal law, (5) debts and taxes due under other New Mexico laws, and (6) all other debts.

When creditors must present claims:

Within two months after executor first published notice, or within three years after the deceased's death if no notice.

State taxes:

Estate tax plus an additional tax based upon federal estate tax's state tax credit.

New York

Claims with priority:

(1) Administrative expenses, (2) funeral expenses, (3) debts with preference under federal and New York State laws, (4) property taxes assessed against deceased prior to death, (5) judgments and decrees against deceased from prior to death, and (6) all other debts.

When creditors must present claims:

Within three months after executor first published notice, or within seven months after the executor's appointment if no notice.

State taxes:

Estate tax plus an additional tax based upon federal estate tax's state tax credit.

North Carolina

Claims with priority:

(1) Debts which by law are secured by a lien on specific property (preference is not to exceed the value of that property, however), (2) up to $2,000 in funeral expenses, (3) debts and taxes with preference under federal law, (4) debts and taxes with preference under North Carolina law, (5) judgments rendered against deceased prior to death, (6) employees' wages and last-illness expenses from one year prior to date of deceased's death, and (7) all other debts.

When creditors must present claims:

Within six months after executor first published notice, or within three years after the deceased's death if no notice.

State taxes:

Inheritance tax based on the federal estate tax's state tax credit.

NORTH DAKOTA

Claims with priority:
(1) Administrative expenses, (2) funeral expenses, (3) debts and taxes with preference under federal law, (4) expenses during last sickness, (5) debts and taxes with preference under state law, and (6) all other debts.

When creditors must present claims:
Within three months after executor first published notice, or within three years after the deceased's death if no notice.

State taxes:
Estate tax plus an additional tax based upon federal estate tax's state tax credit.

OHIO

Claims with priority:
(1) Administrative expenses, (2) $2,000 in funeral expenses, (3) allowance to surviving spouse and children, (4) debts with preference under federal law, (5) last illness expenses, (6) an additional $1,000 for funeral expenses not covered by priority 2, (7) debts and taxes with preference under Ohio law, (8) debts for manual labor performed for deceased from one year prior to date of death, but no more than $300 per person, and (9) all other debts.

When creditors must present claims:
Within three months after executor was appointed.

State taxes:
Estate tax plus an additional tax based upon federal estate tax's state tax credit.

OKLAHOMA

Claims with priority:
(1) Funeral expenses, (2) last-illness expenses, (3) court allowances to the family, (4) taxes due to the U.S., Oklahoma, or any locality, (5) debts with preference under federal or Oklahoma law, (6) judgments and other liens rendered against the deceased prior to death, and (7) all other debts.

When creditors must present claims:
Usually within two months after executor first published notice.

State taxes:
Estate tax plus an additional tax based upon federal estate tax's state tax credit.

OREGON

Claims with priority:
(1) Family allowances, (2) administrative expenses, (3) funeral expenses, (4) debts and taxes with preference under federal law, (5) last-illness expenses, (6) taxes with preference under Oregon law, (7) certain miscellaneous debts, and (8) all other debts.

When creditors must present claims:
Within four months after executor first published notice.

State taxes:
Estate tax plus an additional tax based upon federal estate tax's state tax credit.

PENNSYLVANIA

Claims with priority:
(1) Administrative expenses, (2) family exemptions, (3) various medical expenses from six months prior to death and funeral expenses, (4) cost of tombstone, (5) rent owed by deceased from six months prior to death, and (6) all other debts.

When creditors must present claims:
Within one year after the date of death.

State taxes:
Inheritance tax based on the federal estate tax's state tax credit.

RHODE ISLAND

Claims with priority:
(1) Administrative expenses, (2) funeral expenses, (3) last-illness expenses, (4) debts to the U.S., (5) debts and taxes with preference under Rhode Island law, (6) wages due to employees of deceased from six months prior to date of death, but no more than $100 per person, and (7) all other debts.

When creditors must present claims:
Within six months after clerk of court first published notice.

State taxes:
Estate tax plus an additional tax based upon federal estate tax's state tax credit.

SOUTH CAROLINA

Claims with priority:
(1) Administrative expenses and funeral expenses, (2) last-illness expenses, (3) debts and taxes with preference under federal law, (4) debts and taxes with preference under South Carolina law, and (5) all other debts.

When creditors must present claims:
Within eight months after executor first published notice.

State taxes:
Estate tax plus an additional tax based upon federal estate tax's state tax credit.

SOUTH DAKOTA

Claims with priority:
(1) Administrative expenses, (2) funeral expenses, (3) last-illness expenses, (4) debts to servants and employees for services from 60 days prior to death, (5) debts with preference under federal law, and (6) all other debts.

When creditors mast present claims:
Within four months after executor first published notice, or within three years after the deceased's death if no notice.

State taxes:
Inheritance tax based on the federal estate tax's state tax credit.

TENNESSEE

Claims with priority:
(1) Administrative expenses, (2) federal and state taxes, (3) funeral expenses, and (4) all other debts.

When creditors must present claims:
Within six months after executor published notice, or within one year after the deceased's death if no notice.

State taxes:
Inheritance tax based on the federal estate tax's state tax credit.

TEXAS

Claims with priority:
(1) Funeral expenses and last-illness expenses, not to exceed $5,000, (2) administrative expenses, (3) tax liens and other secured liens, (4) various Texas state tax debts, and (5) all other debts.

When creditors must present claims:
Within six months after executor was appointed.

State taxes:
Estate tax plus an additional tax based upon federal estate tax's state tax credit.

UTAH

Claims with priority:
(1) Funeral expenses, (2) administrative expenses, (3) debts and taxes with preference under federal law, (4) last-illness expenses, (5) debts and taxes with preference under Utah law, and (6) all other debts.

When creditors must present claims:
Within three months after executor first published notice, or within three years after the deceased's death if no notice.

State taxes:
Estate tax plus an additional tax based upon federal estate tax's state tax credit.

VERMONT

Claims with priority:
(1) Administrative expenses, (2) funeral expenses up to $1,000 and last-illness expenses, (3) wages due to deceased's employees from three months before death up to $300 per person, and (4) all other claims.

When creditors must present claims:
Within four months after executor first published notice, or within three years after the deceased's death if no notice.

State taxes:
Estate tax plus an additional tax based upon federal estate tax's state tax credit.

VIRGIN ISLANDS

Claims with priority:

(1) Administrative expenses, (2) funeral expenses, (3) taxes, (4) last-illness expenses, (5) debts with preference under federal or Virgin Islands law, (6) debts secured by liens on the deceased's property, (7) debts due to the deceased's employees, and (8) all other claims.

When creditors must present claims:

Within six months after executor published notice.

State taxes:

Estate tax plus an additional tax based upon federal estate tax's state tax credit.

VIRGINIA

Claims with priority:

(1) Administrative expenses, (2) family allowances, (3) funeral expenses up to $500, (4) debts and taxes with preference under federal law, (5) last-illness expenses up to $400 per hospital and $150 per person, (6) debts to the State of Virginia, (7) any debts the deceased had in any capacity as a trustee or fiduciary, and (8) all other debts.

When creditors must present claims:

Within one year after being notified or by a "hearing to show cause" following executor's appointment.

State taxes:

Estate tax plus an additional tax based upon federal estate tax's state tax credit.

WASHINGTON

Claims with priority:

(1) Administrative expenses, (2) funeral expenses, (3) last-illness expenses, (4) wages due to deceased's employees from 60 days prior to death, (5) debts with preference under federal law, (6) taxes, or any debts to the State of Washington, (7) judgments against deceased from prior to death and which are liens against the deceased's real estate, and (8) all other debts.

When creditors must present claims:

Within four months after executor published notice, or within eighteen months after the deceased's death if no notice.

State taxes:

Estate tax plus an additional tax based upon federal estate tax's state tax credit.

WEST VIRGINIA

Claims with priority:

(1) Administrative expenses, (2) funeral expenses up to $600, (3) up to $100 per creditor for last-illness expenses, (4) debts to the U.S., (5) debts to the State of West Virginia, (6) taxes, (7) any debts incurred by deceased in serving as a trustee or in a similar function, and (8) all other debts.

When creditors must present claims:

Within two to three months after executor published notice.

State taxes:

Estate tax plus an additional tax based upon federal estate tax's state tax credit.

WISCONSIN

Claims with priority:

(1) Administrative expenses, (2) funeral expenses, (3) family allowances, (4) last-illness expenses, (5) debts to federal, state, or local authorities, (6) wages to deceased's employees from three months prior to death up to $300 per employee, (7) up to $10,000 in property for the spouse which the court can order, and (8) all other claims.

When creditors must present claims:

Within three to four months after court issues an order to creditors directing them to present their claims.

State taxes:

Estate tax plus an additional tax based upon federal estate tax's state tax credit.

WYOMING

Claims with priority:

(1) Court costs, (2) administrative expenses, (3) funeral expenses, (4) allowances for surviving spouse and children, (5) debts and taxes with preference under federal law, (6) last-illness expenses, (7) taxes with preference under Wyoming law, and (8) other miscellaneous creditors and all other debts.

When creditors must present claims:

Within three months after executor first published notice.

State taxes:

Estate tax plus an additional tax based upon federal estate tax's state tax credit.

MANAGING THE ESTATE

Most estates require very little managing in the form of personal, day-to-day management. While you're paying off claims or selling estate assets, you simply keep the estate's money in the estate account and keep important documents such as stock and bond certificates in a safe place such as a safe deposit box. If there's real estate in the estate, you need to make sure that it's properly maintained and that all necessary repairs are made. For a small fee, typically 8 percent of the monthly rent, payable out of the estate, you can usually hire a professional property-management firm to take care of these responsibilities for you. Check the Yellow Pages under Real Estate Management for names and numbers. In order to fulfill your fiduciary duty to the estate, you should call several firms, compare their fee quotations, and ask for references before making your choice.

The law usually gives you broad powers to do what you think is best in managing the estate, so long as your actions are reasonable and you make a good-faith effort to act in the best interests of the heirs and beneficiaries. This chapter's appendix gives a summary of every state's legal principles concerning executor powers. A typical summary will say that the executor has "broad powers to sell property, pay debts, and manage estate, so long as the executor acts reasonably for the benefit of interested persons." Of course, you'll come across variations on this theme.

However, before selling any real estate, business interest, copyright or patent interest, or any other estate property whose value cannot be immediately and obviously determined in dollars and cents (like stocks and bonds traded on national exchanges, for which you can get daily price quotes in the newspaper), you should check with the local courthouse's clerk's office first. Ask whether you need to get prior court approval. You need to check because the court may want to (1) give the heirs or beneficiaries a chance to object if they wish to, (2) compare the appraisal, if any, for the property that you submitted with the inventory to the sales price of the property and determine whether the sale is for a fair price, or (3) make sure that there's no conflict of interest, such as if you were selling a piece of land belonging to the estate to a real estate development company that your spouse or a close relative works for.

Another important limitation on your powers as executor was discussed in Chapter 5. This is the list of creditor-priority categories established by state law if the estate doesn't have enough money to pay all creditors. If the estate is insolvent, you must pay off the claimants according to their priority category or you could be held personally liable for the debt.

The Deceased's Business.

The most common exception to the rule that estates don't require much management is when the deceased has left behind a business. It could be a family business, such as a store, or a personal business enterprise, such as a doctor's professional medical practice. In Issue 5 of Chapter 1, I discussed the various types of business entities. Now, you have to determine whether you will (1) run the business or (2) sell it.

The law presumes that you must sell the business and distribute the proceeds to the heirs or beneficiaries unless the will gives you specific authority to run the business or specific instructions to pass it on intact. If the will gave you authority to run the business or instructed you to pass it on intact, you should (1) check with the clerk's office to see what court procedures, if any, you must comply with and (2) consider the following factors and decide whether you should get a professional to manage the business for you and for the estate.

1. *Are you qualified to run the business?* Do you have the necessary business, managerial, technical, or professional expertise to run it and run it profitably? Even if you do, do you have all of the necessary state licenses and certificates? Finally, do you have the time to spend, given your personal job and family commitments?

2. *Are there others connected with the business who could run it as well or better than you?* For example, there might be capable senior employees, managers, the deceased's spouse, or family members. If you pick someone to run the business who is an heir or a beneficiary, such as the deceased's spouse or a family member, you have to be certain that he or she will run the business for the benefit of *all* heirs and beneficiaries, not just him or herself.

3. *Is there a buyout agreement, as discussed in Issue 5 of Chapter 1?* If other persons with an interest in the business have the right to buy out the deceased's interest, you may have to ask the court for permission to ignore any conflicting provision in the will, such as a provision instructing you to pass the business on to the beneficiaries.

4. ***Is the business located out-of-state or are there any significant business operations or properties out-of-state?*** If so, you may have to get an ancillary Co-Personal Representative in every one of such other states.

Finally, if you do wind up getting a third party to run the business, make sure they comply with any court-imposed bonding requirement. Ask the clerk's office (1) what, if any, bond is required, (2) what a third party has to do to qualify, and (3) what you personally are required to do in the process. If the third party promises to get a bond, but doesn't do it, you could be found negligent for not having followed up and made sure that they complied with the law.

Selling the Business

If you have to sell the business, then the selling process itself gives you significant responsibilities because of your fiduciary duty to the estate and to the heirs or beneficiaries. First, since a business is precisely the type of estate asset discussed above where prior court approval before sale may be necessary, before you sell it you must check with the clerk's office. Otherwise, you could get into trouble for selling it without court approval.

Here is a summary of the three basic steps involved if you have to sell the deceased's business.

1. ***Have the Business Appraised.*** If you haven't already done so in connection with the inventory and appraisal deadlines, get a professional appraiser to appraise the business. This appraisal will give you a yardstick by which to measure any purchase offers. Further, if the beneficiaries ever challenge your actions, the valuation could help to protect you if the sales price was near or above the valuation amount.

2. ***Identify Possible Buyers.*** Unless the deceased was a multimillionaire, any business he or she left behind was a small business. There is no regular market for the sale of a small business. Even if the business was a corporation, the stock was probably owned by only the deceased and a few other people, and not traded on a national exchange. Therefore, you may have to do some digging for possible buyers. First, check the various business documents discussed in Issue 5 of Chapter 1. It may be that any buyout provision works in favor of the deceased, meaning that you can force the deceased's business partners to pay a fair price (which the appraisal will help determine) for the deceased's share of the business. You may want to get a lawyer to help you understand the legalese.

   Even if there's no buyout provision, the deceased's business partners or the corporation's other stockholders are logical buyers. They will understand the business, appreciate what went into the appraisal, and will not want to see part of their business sold to a stranger. Consider approaching them about buying out the deceased's interest. If the deceased's business has no partners or other stockholders, some other potential buyers may include (1) senior managers and/or employees or (2) one or more of the heirs or beneficiaries.

You could try approaching these possible buyers on your own, or through a professional. There are people who specialize in brokering the sales of businesses, but you have to be careful in using one. Usually such "business brokers" are not regulated, or if they are, the degree of regulation is minimal at best. They may charge you a flat fee for their services, regardless of whether they get a sale, or they may take a percentage of the final sales price as their fee.

Of course, a business broker may be able to get a better price because of his or her negotiating experience and business expertise. In addition, a business broker may be able to develop leads and potential buyers if none of the obvious buyers listed above works out. Therefore, my advice to you concerning business brokers is to shop around and get a feel for the rates that they charge. I prefer business brokers whose only fee is a percentage of the sales price, since this ensures their interest in getting the business sold. Ask for references, and make sure that their "contingency fee" doesn't exceed what is customary for business brokers in the area. After you've chosen a business broker, have a lawyer review the contracts, other documents, and terms of sale before you accept any offer. You should also have a lawyer review any agreement that the business broker wants you to sign before he or she will help you.

3. *Examine the Terms of the Offer.* If you get an offer to buy the business, whether or not through a business broker, take a close look at the terms of the offer. If you've obtained a lawyer, he or she can help you. Obviously, the purchase price is an important term, but so are these questions:

   (a) Is the purchase price a lump sum, to be paid all at once and up front when the papers are signed, or is it to be paid over time?

   (b) If the purchase price is over time, is the buyer offering collateral as security? Collateral could be a letter of credit with a bank, a lien on the business's assets, or a right to foreclose on the business.

   (c) Are there any "contingencies" in the documents concerning the buyer's obligation to purchase the business? "Contingencies" is legalese for loopholes that may let the buyer back out at the last minute.

   (d) What kind of warranties, representations, indemnities, and/or guaranties are you and/or the estate required to give to the buyer? The fewer the better, and preferably none at all.

(e) If the deceased's business was a corporation, is it being sold through a *stock purchase and sale agreement,* or through an *asset purchase and sale agreement?* Check with the accountant and the lawyer because there are important tax and legal differences between the two.

(f) Is there any conflict among the interests of heirs or beneficiaries with respect to the terms of sale? For example, what if some beneficiaries work for the business and can be fired by the new owner, but others need cash as soon as possible? You have to try to accommodate their interests as best you can. Try to get all the beneficiaries to consent in writing (the lawyer can give you a form) before accepting any offer.

A Final Word.

If the business has been losing money or is otherwise in danger of going broke, consider seeing a bankruptcy lawyer. Federal bankruptcy laws may be able to protect the business from being eaten up by its creditors, who may or may not also be creditors of the deceased. There is also a state version of federal bankruptcy protection, called "assignment for the benefit of creditors," which may or may not be preferable to federal law. The estate cannot declare bankruptcy, but the business can, although if the business was a sole proprietorship it might have to be incorporated first so that it is a legal business entity distinct from the estate.

Before leaving this chapter, take a look at the summary form of asset purchase and sale agreement which begins on page 130. Although you should follow my advice and get a lawyer to assist you with the sale of the deceased's business, in legal matters it always pays to have some form of your own to refer to. Therefore, for your reference, I have included a very shortened version of the standard asset purchase and sale agreement that I use in my legal practice. It differs only slightly from its legal cousin, the stock purchase and sale agreement, which I mentioned previously.

ASSET PURCHASE AND SALE AGREEMENT

THIS ASSET PURCHASE AND SALE AGREEMENT, dated _____ ,
200 ___ , is by and among _____ *[insert name of deceased's business]* _____ ,
a _____ *[insert state]* _____ corporation
(the "Company"); _____ , executor of the
estate of, _____ the beneficiaries of
said estate, namely __ , _____ (sometimes referred
to herein and jointly as "Sellers") and _____ *[insert name of purchaser]* _____ I N C.,
a _____ *[insert state]* _____ corporation, ("PURCHASER").

RECITALS

WHEREAS the parties hereto desire to set forth herein the terms and conditions
pertaining to the purchase and sale of the ongoing business operations and assets of
the Company as herein described;

NOW, THEREFORE in consideration of the mutual premises herein contained
and other valuable consideration, receipt and sufficiency of which is hereby acknowledged, and intending to be legally bound hereby, the parties hereto covenant and agree
as follows:

SECTION 1
DEFINITIONS

1.1 *Defined Terms.* In addition to other terms defined throughout this Agreement, the following terms shall have the following meanings when used in this
Agreement:

(a) "Agreement" shall mean this Asset Purchase and Sale Agreement.

(b) "Assets" shall mean the ongoing business operations of the Company
which consists of all assets of the Company, tangible and intangible, current or non-
current, including but not limited to the name of the Company and assets set forth
on the List referred to in Section 4.3(ii) below and excluding all liabilities of Company and Sellers whether contingent, undisclosed or otherwise, if not expressly included hereunder.

(c) "Business Property Rights" shall mean all technology, patents, copyrights,
trademarks, trade names, service marks (and any applications for any of the foregoing)
and trade secrets used by the Company.

(d) "Closing" or "Closing Date" shall mean the date upon which the transactions contemplated by the terms of the Agreement are consummated.

(e) "Company" shall mean _____ I n c.,
a _____ corporation, and any successor
thereto which assumes the obligations of the Company set forth in this Agreement.

(f) "IRS Rules" shall mean the Internal Revenue Code, as amended, and
the Rules and Regulations promulgated by the Internal Revenue Service pursuant to
its authority under Title 26 of the U.S. Code.

SECTION 2
SALE OF THE ASSETS

2.1 Sale of the Assets. Subject to the terms and conditions hereof, the Company hereby sells to the Purchaser, and the Purchaser hereby purchases from the Company, all of the Company's right, title and interest in and to the Assets for the following consideration (collectively, the "Purchase Price"):

Payment of $_____ in immediately available funds at Closing; *[Insert any other terms]*

SECTION 3
CLOSING DATE; DELIVERY

3.1 *Closing Date.* The Closing of the purchase and sale of the Assets shall be effected at the offices of _____ *[insert name of lawyer you hired or other such person]* _____ on _____ , 200 ___ , or at such place and on any other date or place mutually acceptable to all parties.

3.2 *Deliveries at the Closing.* Subject to the conditions set forth in this Agreement, at the Closing Sellers and the Company shall deliver all other documents required to be delivered by them at or prior to the Closing or otherwise required by Purchaser in connection herewith, against (a) payment by Purchaser to Sellers of the Purchase Price and (b) delivery by Purchaser to Sellers or Company of any other documents required to be delivered by Purchaser at or prior to the Closing or otherwise required in connection herewith.

SECTION 4
CONDITIONS TO CLOSING

The Purchaser's obligation to purchase the Assets at Closing is subject to the fulfillment to Purchaser's satisfaction, on or prior to Closing, of the following conditions:

4.1 *Representations and Warranties.* Sellers and the Company, either individually or jointly, shall not be in breach of any representation or warranty made in this Agreement.

4.2 *Liabilities.* The Company shall have not incurred any liability, direct or contingent (as the term is ordinarily used), other than as set forth in its financial statements dated _____ 200 ___ , and in the List, as hereinafter defined, other than ordinary and necessary business expenses incurred in the ordinary course of business.

4.3 *Assets and Liabilities.* Sellers and Company shall deliver to Purchaser a list of all of the Company's assets and liabilities or obligations (the "List") as of, _____ , 200 ___ . Sellers and Company hereby certify as to the accuracy and completeness of the List, and hereby represent and warrant that there will be no material change in the assets, liabilities or obligations described on the List and the accuracy and completeness of the description thereof between _____ 200 ___ , and the Closing Date.

(i) The Liabilities or obligations of the Company described in the List shall include, but are not limited to, the following:

(a) All material commitments of the Company including purchases or leases of realty or personalty;

(b) All employment contracts and collective bargaining arrangements;

(c) All promissory notes wherein the Company is the promisor or is a guarantor;

(d) Any and all life insurance, pension, deferred compensation, medical reimbursement, retirement payment, profit sharing, or other benefit arrangements;

(e) Actions pending or threatened against or involving the Company; and

(f) Any vested or contingent Federal, state, or local tax lien or liability.

(ii) The Assets of the Company described in the List shall include, but are not limited to, the following:

(a) all items of furniture, fixtures, and equipment of Company;

(b) all files and records related to the operation of the company;

(c) all prepaid expenses of Company;

(d) rights arising under contracts accepted by Purchaser to the extent assignable;

(e) the use of any corporate name, trade name, or assumed name of the Company and any variation thereof, the Company's existing directory listings and advertisements therefor, telephone numbers, customer lists, and all other current records necessary for Purchaser's operation of the business:

(f) work in process, inventory of supplies and art goods, other inventory, and all accounts receivable due and payable to the Company or billed by the Company, but not yet due and payable, or not yet billed by the Company in respect of services performed, or goods sold by, the Company up and to the Closing Date;

(g) all Business Property Rights: and

(h) any and all Goodwill.

4.4 *Bill of Sale.* A duly executed Bill of Sale in a form reasonably acceptable to Purchaser's counsel for the Assets listed on the List.

4.5 *Consents.* Sellers, Company and Purchaser, shall have obtained any and all third party consents necessary for the parties to consummate the transactions contemplated by this Agreement.

SECTION 5
MISCELLANEOUS

5.1 *Titles and Captions.* All section titles or captions in this Agreement are for convenience only. They shall not be deemed part of this Agreement and shall in no way define, limit, extend or describe the scope or intent of provisions herein.

5.2 *Applicable Law.* This Agreement is to be governed by, and construed, interpreted, and enforced in accordance with the laws of the State of _____
____*[insert deceased's state]*____ , as amended, and the rules and regulations promulgated thereunder.

5.3. *Binding Effect and Assignment.* This Agreement shall be binding upon and inure to the benefit of the successors and assigns of the parties.

5.4 *Notices.* All notices, requests, instructions, or other documents required hereunder shall be deemed to have been given or made when mailed by registered mail or certified mail, return receipt requested, postage prepaid to:

If the COMPANY, then:

[Insert Address]

If the SELLERS, then:

[Insert Address]

If the PURCHASER, then:

[Insert Address]

Any party may from time to time give the others written notice of a change in the address to which notices are to be sent and of any successors in interest.

5.5 *Severability.* Inapplicability or unenforceability of any provision of this Agreement shall not impair the operation or validity of any other provision hereof. If any provision shall be declared inapplicable or unenforceable, there shall be added automatically as part of this Agreement a provision as similar in terms to such inapplicable or unenforceable provision as may be possible and be legal, valid and enforceable.

5.6 *Entire Agreement.* This Agreement constitutes the entire agreement among the parties hereto pertaining to the subject matter hereof, and supersedes all prior agreements and understandings pertaining thereto. No covenant, representation, or condition not expressed in this Agreement shall affect or be deemed to interpret, change or restrict the express provisions hereof and no amendments hereto shall be valid unless made in writing and signed by all parties hereto.

5.7 *Payment of Attorneys' Fees.* Purchaser shall bear the cost of both parties' reasonable attorneys' fees.

IN WITNESS WHEREOF the parties hereto have executed this Agreement on the day and year first above written.

COMPANY

_____

By: _____
Its: _____

SELLERS:

_____

_____

_____

By: _____
Its: _____

PURCHASER

_____

By: _____
Its: _____

APPENDIX SIX

Fifty-state summary of executor powers. Includes the District of Columbia and the Virgin Islands. State laws change periodically, so be certain to confirm the information set forth below concerning your state with an authoritative source, such as the court clerk's office or if necessary an attorney.

ALABAMA

Broad powers to sell property, pay debts, and manage estate. Executor is subject to a "prudent person" rule in making investment and management decisions.

ALASKA

Broad powers to sell property, pay debts, and manage estate, so long as the executor acts reasonably for the benefit of interested persons.

ARIZONA

Limited only by the standard of care and duty of accounting applicable to trustees.

ARKANSAS

If the will does not expressly give the executor certain fiduciary and other powers, there are important limitations on the executor's powers. For example, if the will doesn't give the executor a "power of sale," then both real property and personal property can be sold only with a court order. For the most part the will must refer to specific provisions of the Arkansas Code in order to effectively give the executor more powers, so be careful.

CALIFORNIA

Certain actions require court approval beforehand, such as executing notes, executing leases and mortgages, selling property, continuing the deceased's business, or agreeing to out-of-court settlements in legal matters against the estate.

COLORADO

Broad powers to sell property, pay debts, and manage estate, so long as the executor acts reasonably for the benefit of interested persons.

CONNECTICUT

The deceased's will can give the executor some very broad powers if it refers to certain key provisions of the Connecticut General Statutes.

DELAWARE

Broad powers to sell property, pay debts, and manage estate, so long as the executor acts reasonably for the benefit of interested persons.

DISTRICT OF COLUMBIA

Broad powers to sell property, pay debts, and manage estate, so long as the executor acts reasonably for the benefit of interested persons.

FLORIDA

Will should give the executor a power of sale or it may be necessary to get a court order to sell property.

GEORGIA

Wills, trust agreement, and other documents can give the executor extensive fiduciary powers, but must refer to special sections of the Official Code of Georgia.

HAWAII

Selling, mortgaging, or leasing estate assets requires prior court approval.

IDAHO

Broad powers to sell property, pay debts, and manage estate, so long as the executor acts reasonably for the benefit of interested persons.

ILLINOIS

Executor needs prior court approval to sell or mortgage real estate.

INDIANA

If the will doesn't give the executor the power to sell estate property, the executor must get a court order before doing so.

Iowa

Broad powers to sell property, pay debts, and manage estate, so long as the executor acts reasonably for the benefit of interested persons.

Kansas

Broad powers to sell property, pay debts, and manage estate, so long as the executor acts reasonably for the benefit of interested persons.

Kentucky

Broad powers to sell property, pay debts, and manage estate, so long as the executor acts reasonably for the benefit of interested persons. If the will does not expressly give the executor the power to sell real estate, the executor must get prior court approval.

Louisiana

Somewhat limited. The executor needs prior court approval for a variety of matters, including paying any debts and selling or leasing estate property.

Maine

Broad powers to sell property, pay debts, and manage estate, so long as the executor acts reasonably for the benefit of interested persons.

Maryland

Broad powers to sell property, pay debts, and manage estate, so long as the executor acts reasonably for the benefit of interested persons.

Massachusetts

Must get prior consent of court to sell or lease real estate.

Michigan

Executor can mortgage or pledge estate assets only with prior court approval.

Minnesota

Broad powers to manage estate so long as the executor acts reasonably for the benefit of interested persons.

Mississippi

Broad powers to manage estate so long as the executor acts reasonably for the benefit of interested persons.

Missouri

Broad powers to manage estate so long as the executor acts reasonably for the benefit of interested persons.

MONTANA

All sales of estate property must be conducted fairly and for the best price obtainable.

NEBRASKA

Broad powers to manage estate so long as the executor acts reasonably for the benefit of interested persons.

NEVADA

Broad powers to manage estate so long as the executor acts reasonably for the benefit of interested persons.

NEW HAMPSHIRE

Broad powers to manage estate so long as the executor acts reasonably for the benefit of interested persons.

NEW JERSEY

Broad powers to manage estate so long as the executor acts reasonably for the benefit of interested persons.

NEW MEXICO

Must have prior court approval before exchanging or abandoning estate property such as real estate, paying off charitable pledges made by the deceased, or if executor does not plan to take security for the unpaid balance of any estate sale.

NEW YORK

Broad powers to manage estate so long as the executor acts reasonably for the benefit of interested persons.

NORTH CAROLINA

Broad powers to manage estate so long as the executor acts reasonably for the benefit of interested persons.

NORTH DAKOTA

Broad powers to manage estate so long as the executor acts reasonably for the benefit of interested persons.

OHIO

Executor cannot invest estate monies without express clause in will authorizing him or her to make investments, or prior court approval.

OKLAHOMA

Executor must get prior court approval before leasing any estate lands for oil, gas, or mineral exploitation.

OREGON

Broad powers to manage estate so long as the executor acts reasonably for the benefit of interested persons.

PENNSYLVANIA

Must get prior court approval before pledging or mortgaging any real estate or personal property of the estate.

RHODE ISLAND

Prior court approval required before the executor can keep the deceased's business running or before the executor can lease out estate property, invest estate money, or take certain other important actions.

SOUTH CAROLINA

Broad powers to manage estate so long as the executor acts reasonably for the benefit of interested persons. Executor's power to make investments, however, is subject to statutory and court regulation.

SOUTH DAKOTA

Broad powers to manage estate so long as the executor acts reasonably for the benefit of interested persons.

TENNESSEE

Broad powers to manage estate so long as the executor acts reasonably for the benefit of interested persons. However, most executors get court orders authorizing their actions in order to safeguard themselves.

TEXAS

Broad powers to manage estate so long as the executor acts reasonably for the benefit of interested persons.

UTAH

Broad powers to manage estate so long as the executor acts reasonably for the benefit of interested persons.

VERMONT

Executor usually needs prior court approval before selling real estate or personal property of the estate.

VIRGIN ISLANDS

Executor must get prior court approval before selling any personal property or real property from the estate.

VIRGINIA

Broad powers to manage estate so long as the executor acts reasonably for the benefit of interested persons.

WASHINGTON

Broad powers to manage estate so long as the executor acts reasonably for the benefit of interested persons. Executor needs prior court approval before he or she can sell, lease, or mortgage any of the real property or personal property of the estate.

WEST VIRGINIA

Cannot sell estate property contrary to the terms of the will unless sale is to pay for administrative costs, funeral expenses, or other debts.

WISCONSIN

Broad powers to manage estate so long as the executor acts reasonably for the benefit of interested persons.

WYOMING

Broad powers to manage estate so long as the executor acts reasonably for the benefit of interested persons. Must have prior court approval before selling, leasing, or mortgaging any estate property.

Accountings, Distributions to Beneficiaries, and Closing the Estate

This chapter covers your last three major duties as the executor. They are to (1) submit a paper accounting to the court, (2) distribute what's left in the estate after claimants and taxes have been paid, and (3) close the estate.

Accountings

In Chapter 4, I discussed the estate inventory and your duty to gather, appraise, and report to the court all of the estate's assets. In the accounting, you report to the court what has happened to those assets since you filed the inventory: how much was paid out in claims, how much was earned in interest on the estate account, whether the sales price for a particular piece of property was more or less than its appraised value, and so forth. There are three types of accountings.

(i) The First and Final Accounting. If the estate had no real estate or personal property to be sold, no business of the deceased to be liquidated, and no creditor complications, it may be that the first accounting is also the final accounting. Check with the local courthouse's clerk's office about when the accounting is due, and get the necessary forms. If all the estate

creditors have been paid off and any other business of the estate has been accomplished by the first accounting's deadline, then all that remains is for any taxes, administrative costs, attorneys' fees, and your executor fees to be paid before what's left can be distributed to the heirs or beneficiaries. This "first and final accounting" is the simplest, most common, and best type of accounting for you.

(ii) Periodic Accountings. There may be assets in the estate, such as the deceased's business, real estate, or some other property, that you haven't been able to sell by the filing deadline for the first accounting. If so, then you may have to file additional accountings every six or 12 months thereafter until all such property has finally been sold. Check with the clerk's office concerning the relevant time period for such "periodic accountings." There may be other reasons for having to file periodic accountings, such as legal actions against the estate by claimants, heirs, beneficiaries, or the deceased's spouse, which make it impossible to distribute the estate until the dispute is resolved in the courts.

(iii) Small-Estate Accountings. If the estate is a small estate, the accounting procedure will likely be much simpler and much more informal. Again, the clerk's office can give you details.

For all accountings

You cannot make the final distributions to the heirs or beneficiaries until you have filed the accounting(s) with the court and the court gives its approval.

A sample form of accounting is on page 147. Usually the clerk's office will provide you with the necessary forms, although sometimes they simply give you instructions on how to prepare your own. In order to give an accurate accounting, you will need to have maintained a scrupulously accurate estate checkbook and ledger, as well as having kept all bills, receipts, and other relevant documents. As discussed in Chapter 5, accountants' fees are usually priority administrative expenses that can be paid out of the estate, so you should definitely consider using a CPA to help you prepare the accounting.

Fee petitions with the accounting

In addition to final distributions to the heirs or beneficiaries, you may need the court's permission before paying (1) accountants' fees, (2) attorneys' fees, and (3) the fees you are entitled to for your services as executor. Check with the clerk's office about whether there must be detailed descriptions of services rendered, called *petitions,* with the accounting before (1) and (2) can be paid. If the answer is yes, the accountants and/or the lawyers are responsible for providing you with the necessary petition to go with the accounting. Why are such petitions required? Because the courts want to be sure that the accountants and the lawyers don't abuse their priority creditor status and milk the estate.

The following accounting was done under the laws of "State X" in accordance with its hypothetical creditor-priority categories as follows: (1) administrative expenses, (2) funeral expenses, (3) last-illness expenses, and (4) all other creditors. It also assumes, for purposes of illustration only, that the original inventory had reported $50,000 in estate assets.

State laws differ with respect to the executor's fees you are entitled to—this chapter's appendix summarizes all of them. Although most states treat your executor's fees as a priority administrative expense if the estate is insolvent, states differ concerning the size of your fees. For example, many states let the local courts and local practice determine what you get. The appendix's summary of Nebraska law is typical: "An unspecified amount of 'reasonable compensation,'" meaning that it will depend on local practice and the particular judge.

Therefore, in states like Nebraska, it is likely that you will have to prepare a petition describing in detail what you did as executor. The more difficult the estate was to administer, such as in the case of a deceased's business or litigation involving the estate, the larger your court-approved fees are likely to be. In other states, however, your executor fees are fixed. For example, in Nevada: "Executor gets 4% of the first $15,000 of the estate, 3% of the next $85,000, and 2% of everything over $100,000."

You may have to file a petition in states like Nevada, but the detail required will probably be less, since the local courts don't have as much influence.

One final note. If an accounting has errors in it, or the numbers don't add up, the court may order an audit. In an audit, the judge or an official of the court reviews all of the estate records, calculates all of the estate's assets and expenses, and determines what's missing from the accounting. If there is a shortfall, and you don't have any documentation to show where the money went, the court can order you to pay the shortfall to the estate out of your own pocket. Again, consider using a CPA for complicated accountings.

Distributions

Whether it is the first and final accounting or the last periodic accounting, once the court has approved the final accounting, the clerk's office will be able to tell you whether or not you can begin distributing the estate. Often, you cannot begin making distributions until a certain amount of time has passed, during which, heirs and beneficiaries can appeal or contest (1) the court's approval of the accounting or (2) the intended distribution of the estate.

Intestate estates

If the deceased was intestate, then state intestacy laws define who takes what from his or her estate. The people who are entitled to a portion of the deceased's estate are called the heirs. I summarized the spouse's intestate share in Chapter 2, and the clerk's office will be able to tell you who else is entitled to what share. What the spouse doesn't get will be divided up in some manner among the deceased's children, grandchildren, parents, grandparents, and/or other relatives.

Example: In the above accounting for State X, we were left with $34,400 available for distribution. Assume that after all state taxes are paid (there will be no federal tax), $33,000 will be left. The deceased died intestate, and under State X's intestacy laws her husband gets half of her estate. Her children, Bob and Belinda, split the remaining half. Also, assume that you've gotten all necessary court approvals and you can distribute the estate. What do you do?

Answer: You write a check on the estate checking account for $16,500, payable to the order of the deceased's husband. That is his half of the estate. You also give Bob a check for $8,250 and Belinda a check for $8,250. These checks represent their half of the estate, split equally.

Testate estates

As you can see, the intestate estate is usually easy to distribute. So are most testate estates. However, depending on how elaborate the will is, there can be complications. To help you foresee complications and help you figure out how to deal with them, I have set forth some examples below. Remember that the people who are named in the will to receive something from the deceased's estate are called the beneficiaries.

Example: The deceased's will left everything to her husband and "$1,000 each to my children, Bob and Belinda." Bob and Belinda were killed in a car accident before the deceased died, but she never made another will. What happens to the money left to them?

Answer: Bob and Belinda's bequests are said to have *lapsed,* because of their death. Check with the clerk's office or a lawyer about what happens. Usually, the money goes to the other beneficiaries. Here, the deceased's husband would get it. Sometimes, however, the law gives a different answer. For example, if Bob and Belinda had children of their own, then it may be that the children are entitled to the money and not the deceased's husband.

Example: The deceased's will had a clause in it, which says, "I leave my diamond wedding ring, which my grandmother left me, to my daughter Belinda." Unfortunately for Belinda, the deceased sold the ring before she died. What happens to Belinda?

Answer: Belinda's right to the ring has been terminated, or *adeemed.* Belinda can't get any other property of the estate as compensation, either. Depending on the wording of the clause and state law, however, the outcome may be different. If the deceased bought a new wedding ring before she died, and the will simply said, "I leave my wedding ring to my daughter Belinda," then Belinda may be entitled to the new ring.

Example: The deceased's will left $100,000 to her husband, $50,000 to her son Bob, $25,000 to her daughter Belinda, and $25,000 to a local charity. Unfortunately, after taxes and claims, the deceased had only $100,000 left in her estate. This is enough to pay only half the amount that should go to the beneficiaries. Who gets what?

Answer: The answer depends on the state's law of *abatement,* which concerns how beneficiaries are treated if there's not enough money in the estate to give them what the will specified. Check with the clerk's office or a lawyer. In this example, there are several different possible outcomes, depending on the state's laws:

(i) State law says everyone's share is reduced by an equal percentage. In this case, everyone's share would be reduced by 50 percent. The husband gets $50,000, Bob gets $25,000, Belinda gets $12,500, and the charity gets $12,500.

(ii) State law sets up priority categories, in which the first priorities get paid in full, even if it takes all the money in the estate to do. If the husband has priority over everyone else, then the husband gets all $100,000, while Bob, Belinda, and the charity get nothing.

(iii) State law sets up priority categories, but says that in each category the beneficiaries get no more than their prorated share of the estate. Within a category, beneficiaries are paid equally up to but not over their prorated share. In this case, everyone's prorated share means 50 percent. If the husband had first priority, the children second, and the charity last, then this is the result: the husband gets $50,000 (his 50 percent), Bob and Belinda each get $25,000, and the charity gets nothing. Note how this results in Bob's getting only half what he was left in the will, while Belinda gets everything, because the state says they get paid equally until the dollar amount they were left in the will is reached.

(iv) State law is the same as in (iii), except that within each category no one gets more than his or her prorated share. In this case, the husband gets $50,000 (his 50 percent), Bob gets $25,000 (his 50 percent), Belinda gets $12,500 (her 50 percent), and the charity gets $12,500 (its 50 percent).

If there are no complications, then taking care of the testate estate will be as simple as the intestate estate.

Example: In the accounting for State X, we were left with $34,400 available for distribution. Assume that after all state taxes are paid (there will be no federal tax) there will be $33,000 left. The deceased's will said that her husband gets half of her estate and that her children, Bob and Belinda, split the remaining half. Again, assume that you've gotten all necessary court approvals and you can distribute the estate. What do you do?

Answer: As with the intestate estate, you write a check on the estate checking account for $16,500, payable to the order of the deceased's husband. That is his half of the estate. You also give Bob a check for $8,250 and Belinda a check for $8,250. These checks represent their half of the estate, split equally.

A final word concerning property titles

As discussed above, the deceased's will may have left specific items of property to the beneficiaries. Some types of property require documents called *titles,* which are the legal evidence of ownership.

For real estate, the title is a deed, which must be prepared and filed in the land records office of the courthouse for the city or county where the real estate is located. There must be a deed in order to transfer the deceased's real estate to a beneficiary. Ask the clerk's office how to get the proper deed: usually, there's a procedure by which the court can provide you with the proper deed for the beneficiary.

For other types of property, such as cars and boats, the titles are certificates of ownership registered with state authorities. The clerk's office should have forms called *legal heir forms* or *consent to transfer forms* which will enable you to transfer the car, boat, or other property to the beneficiary.

Closing the estate

Once the estate has been distributed to the heirs or beneficiaries, you can close the estate checking account. Further, you should obtain whatever forms or court orders from the clerk's office that are necessary to formally and legally "close," or end, the estate. This is usually a simple matter, and the clerk's office will tell you if anything out of the ordinary, such as a court hearing, is required and how to deal with it. Finally, even after the estate is closed and you have been discharged from your duties as executor, you must keep the estate records in a safe place, such as a safe deposit box or public storage facility, for several years. This is because state law usually gives creditors, claimants, heirs, beneficiaries, and other parties the right to sue you for violating their legal rights for a number of years after the estate is closed. If you get sued, you'll need these records. I recommend that you keep the estate records in a secure place for at least five years, just to be safe.

STATE OF X
ESTATE ACCOUNTING

Estate Number _____

I hereby affirm to all persons that the true and lawful accounting of

_____
(name of deceased)

was filed in the Court of the County of Y, State of X, by

_____
(name of executor)

on the _____ day of _____ 200 ____ , and is as follows:

Item	Income	Disbursement
INCOME		
(1) interest on estate checking account	$2,000	
(2) sale of estate property: appraised at		
$10,000, but sold for $13,000	$3,000	
Total:	$5,000	
DISBURSEMENTS		
(1) administrative expenses		
court fees		$ 500
appraisal costs		$ 500
executor's bond		$ 250
accountants' fees (see attached petition)		$ 1,000
attorneys' fees (see attached petition)		$ 2,000
executor's fees (see attached petition)		$ 1,000
Total:		$ 5,250
(2) funeral expenses		
funeral home		$ 2,000
purchase of burial plot		$ 500
cremation expenses		$ 500
Total:		$ 3,000
(3) last illness expenses		
hospital treatment		$10,000
prescription drugs		$ 275
wheelchair		$ 225
Total:		$10,500
(4) other creditors		
credit card company		$ 1,500
department store		$ 250
electric company		$ 100
Total:		$ 1,850
AMOUNT IN ORIGINAL ESTATE INVENTORY:		$50,000
TOTAL INCOME:		$ 5,000
TOTAL DISBURSEMENTS:		$20,600
TOTAL AMOUNT SUBJECT TO TAXES AND		
AVAILABLE FOR DISTRIBUTION:		$34,400

Appendix Seven

Fifty-state summary of executor compensation. Includes the District of Columbia and the Virgin Islands. State laws change periodically, so be certain to confirm the information set forth below concerning your state with an authoritative source, such as the court clerk's office or if necessary an attorney.

Alabama

Actual expenses and 2 1/2% of the estate.

Alaska

An unspecified amount of "reasonable compensation," meaning that it will depend on local practice and the particular judge.

Arizona

An unspecified amount of "reasonable compensation," meaning that it will depend on local practice and the particular judge.

Arkansas

The executor can get 10% of the first $1,000, 5% of the next $4,000, and 3% of the balance of the value of all estate personal property. The executor can also get an unspecified "reasonable" amount with respect to real estate.

California

Based on the value of the estate: 4% of the first $15,000, 3% on next $85,000, 2% on next $900,000, 1% on next $9,000,000, 0.5% on next $15,000,000, and "reasonable rate" for anything over $25,000,000. As most estates should be under $600,000, remember that California courts will enforce a provision in a will that provides for larger fees.

COLORADO

An unspecified amount of "reasonable compensation," meaning that it will depend on local practice and the particular judge.

CONNECTICUT

An unspecified amount of "reasonable compensation," meaning that it will depend on local practice and the particular judge.

DELAWARE

Set according to a sliding scale determined by the Chancery Court.

DISTRICT OF COLUMBIA

An unspecified amount of "reasonable compensation," meaning that it will depend on local practice and the particular judge.

FLORIDA

Executor gets 6% of the first $1,000 of the estate, 4% of the next $4,000, and 2.5% of everything over $5,000.

GEORGIA

On all money received by the estate, a 2.5% commission, and 2.5% of all money spent by the estate. For property delivered in kind, the judge fixes a "reasonable fee" not to exceed 3% of its value.

HAWAII

Executor is entitled to 4% of the first $15,000 of the estate, 3% of the next $85,000, 2% of the next $900,000, 1.5% of the next $2,000,000, and 1% of any excess over $3,000,000. Further, the executor gets 7% of the first $5,000 in estate annual income and 5% of any income over $5,000.

IDAHO

An unspecified amount of "reasonable compensation," meaning that it will depend on local practice and the particular judge.

ILLINOIS

An unspecified amount of "reasonable compensation," meaning that it will depend on local practice and the particular judge.

INDIANA

An unspecified amount of "just and reasonable compensation," meaning that it will depend on local practice and the particular judge.

IOWA

Up to 6% of the first $1,000 of the estate, 4% of the next $4,000, and 2% of everything over $5,000.

KANSAS

An unspecified amount of "reasonable compensation," meaning that it will depend on local practice and the particular judge.

KENTUCKY

Up to 5% of the value of the personal property in the estate and up to 5% of income collected by the estate.

LOUISIANA

Up to 2% of the value of the estate.

MAINE

An unspecified amount of "reasonable compensation," meaning that it will depend on local practice and the particular judge.

MARYLAND

Up to 10% of first $20,000 and 4% on everything over. Up to 10% of the value of sold real estate. Will can provide for larger fees.

MASSACHUSETTS

Up to 7% of estate income and a sliding-scale percentage of the estate itself which begins at 5% of the first $100,000 and 4% of the next $200,000.

MICHIGAN

An unspecified amount of "reasonable compensation," meaning that it will depend on local practice and the particular judge.

MINNESOTA

An unspecified amount of "reasonable compensation," meaning that it will depend on local practice and the particular judge.

MISSISSIPPI

Up to 7% of the value of the estate.

MISSOURI

Executor gets up to 5% of first $5,000 of the estate, 4% of the next $20,000, 3% of the next $75,000, 2.75% of the next $300,000, 2.5% of the next $600,000, and 2% of anything over $1,000,000.

MONTANA

Executor gets 3% of the first $40,000 of the estate and 2% of everything over $40,000.

NEBRASKA

An unspecified amount of "reasonable compensation," meaning that it will depend on local practice and the particular judge.

NEVADA

Executor gets 4% of the first $15,000 of the estate, 3% of the next $85,000, and 2% of everything over $100,000.

NEW HAMPSHIRE

An unspecified amount of "reasonable compensation," meaning that it will depend on local practice and the particular judge.

NEW JERSEY

Executor gets 5% of the first $200,000 of the estate, 3.5% of the next $800,000, and 2% of everything over. Further, executor gets 6% of estate income.

NEW MEXICO

An unspecified amount of "reasonable compensation," meaning that it will depend on local practice and the particular judge.

NEW YORK

Executor gets 5% of the first $100,000 of the estate, 4% of the next $200,000, 3% of the next $700,000, 2.5% of the next $4,000,000, and 2% of any balance.

NORTH CAROLINA

Executor gets 5% of estate and estate income. Court determines fees if estate worth less than $2,000.

NORTH DAKOTA

An unspecified amount of "reasonable compensation," meaning that it will depend on local practice and the particular judge.

OHIO

Executor gets 4% of the first $100,000 of the estate, 3% of the next $300,000, and 2% of everything over $400,000. The executor gets 1% of the value of any unsold real estate.

OKLAHOMA

Executor gets 5% of the first $1,000 of the estate, 4% of the next $5,000, and 2.5% of everything over.

OREGON

Executor gets up to 7% of the first $1,000 of the estate, 4% of the next $9,000, 3% of the next $40,000, and 2% of everything over $50,000.

PENNSYLVANIA

An unspecified amount of "reasonable compensation," meaning that it will depend on local practice and the particular judge.

RHODE ISLAND

An unspecified amount of "reasonable compensation," meaning that it will depend on local practice and the particular judge.

SOUTH CAROLINA

Executor gets 5% of the estate's assets and estate income.

SOUTH DAKOTA

Executor gets 5% of the first $1,000 of estate personal property and sold real estate, 4% of the next $4,000, and 2.5% of everything over $5,000. If any real estate is not sold, the executor is entitled to "just compensation."

TENNESSEE

An unspecified amount of "reasonable compensation," meaning that it will depend on local practice and the particular judge.

TEXAS

Executor gets up to 5% of all estate income and disbursements.

UTAH

An unspecified amount of "reasonable compensation," meaning that it will depend on local practice and the particular judge.

VERMONT

Executor gets $4 a day. Court may approve additional compensation if the estate involves unusual difficulty or responsibility.

VIRGIN ISLANDS

An unspecified amount of "reasonable compensation," meaning that it will depend on local practice and the particular judge.

VIRGINIA

An unspecified amount of "reasonable compensation," meaning that it will depend on local practice and the particular judge.

WASHINGTON

An unspecified amount of "reasonable compensation," meaning that it will depend on local practice and the particular judge.

WEST VIRGINIA

An unspecified amount of "reasonable compensation," meaning that it will depend on local practice and the particular judge. Executor usually gets 5% of the estate.

WISCONSIN

Executor usually gets up to 2% of the value of the estate.

WYOMING

Executor gets 10% of the first $1,000 of the estate, 5% of the next $4,000, 3% of the next $15,000, and 2% of everything over $20,000.

GLOSSARY OF TERMS

Appraisal: A good-faith estimate of the value of real estate or valuable personal property such as works of art and jewelry.

Appraiser: The person who performs an appraisal. Usually refers to a professional certified by a state agency and/or a private organization, but can also refer to a nonprofessional such as the executor.

Automatic Share, Right of: A spouse's right under state law to a specific share of his or her deceased spouse's estate, regardless of the terms of the will.

Beneficiary: A person who is named in a will to receive something from the deceased's estate.

Claimant: A person, corporation, or other party who files a legal claim asserting a right to property or money from the deceased's estate.

Clerk's Office: The bureaucratic arm of the courts. Every courthouse has a clerk's office to process legal documents, maintain files, and answer questions. Although the clerks are not judges or lawyers, the experience they have in processing the court's paperwork makes them a valuable source of information.

Community Property: A special category of property for married people only that some states have instituted. Both spouses have certain rights in all real estate and personal property acquired by the other during their marriage.

Co-Personal Representative: A sort of "assistant" personal representative in another state, which the personal representative may need in order to administer out-of-state estate property.

Creditor: A person, corporation, or other party who is owed property or money from the deceased's estate. A creditor doesn't become a *claimant* (see definition), however, until he or she files a legal claim.

Deceased/Decedent: The person who has died. These terms are used interchangeably as a generic reference to the dead person, and it doesn't matter whether there's a will or not, unlike more specific terms such as *testator* (see definition).

Distribution: The process by which the estate is given to the *heirs* or *beneficiaries* (see definitions) after all valid claims and taxes are paid.

Election, Right of: A spouse's right under state law to take a certain portion of the estate if the spouse "elects," or chooses, not to take what was left to him or her by the terms of the will.

Estate: The deceased's property, whether real property or personal property.

Executor: Technically refers only to the personal representative for estates where the deceased had a will. Is commonly used as a generic term, however, for all personal representatives.

Fiduciary: A person with a duty, like a trustee, to act for the financial benefit of another or according to the financial instructions of another in a responsible, conservative, and provident manner. If a fiduciary breaches his or her legal duty, he or she can be sued: hence the term "fiduciary duty."

Guardian: The person named in the will to take care of the deceased's children. Although it may be possible for one person to be both personal representative and guardian, legally, the roles include two distinct sets of responsibilities.

Heir: A person entitled to a portion of the deceased's estate if the deceased was intestate.

Intestate: Having died without a will.

Inventory: The list of the deceased's real property and personal property compiled by the personal representative and filed with the court.

Issue: Persons descended from the deceased, including grandchildren and great-grandchildren in addition to children.

Joint Property/Joint Tenancy: Refers to property owned by two or more persons who have *right of survivorship* (see definition). Depending on the state, *real property* (see definition), and/or *personal property* (see definition) may be owned as joint property or as a joint tenancy.

Letters: Generic reference to court orders appointing personal representatives.

Letters of Administration: The court order officially appointing the personal representative of an estate where the deceased was intestate.

Letters Testamentary: The court order officially appointing the personal representative of an estate where the deceased had a will.

Notary Public: A person authorized by the state to officially recognize that documents have been signed and officially seal such documents.

Personal Property: Any property that is not *real property* (see definition).

Personal Representative: A generic term for the person who administers an estate. Also commonly referred to as the executor, although technically an *executor* is not quite the same (see definition).

Petition: A generic term referring to requests made to a court, whether on a preprinted form or in a legal document.

Priority Creditor: One of those *creditors* (see definition) entitled to be paid out of the estate before certain other creditors, provided that they file their claims on time (see definition of *claimant).*

Real Property: Land, buildings, and any other type of real estate, such as condominiums and cooperatives.

Resident Agent: A person or corporation appointed to receive *service of process* (see definition) for the estate and for the executor.

Right of Survivorship: Refers to *joint property/joint tenancy* and *tenancy-by-the-entirety* property (see definitions). When the deceased dies, property automatically becomes the property of the other owners and is never part of the deceased's estate.

Separate Property: Concerns married people only. Refers to those states who have enacted *community-property* (see definition) laws. Some types of property, such as property acquired before getting married, continue to be a spouse's private property during the marriage.

Service of Process: Refers to the delivery of legal papers, such as court documents signaling the beginning of a lawsuit against someone. The legal papers do not have to be delivered to the person actually being sued, but can be sent to his or her *resident agent* (see definition), and usually the law will say that is enough to begin the lawsuit.

Successor Guardian: Someone who becomes the guardian of the deceased's children if the guardian named in the will cannot be the guardian.

Tenancy by the Entirety: Concerns married people only. Tenants by the entirety share property ownership and have *right of survivorship* (see definition). Depending on the state, *real property* (see definition) and/or *personal property* (see definition) may be owned as tenancy by the entireties.

Tenancy in Common: Property owned by two or more people, called tenants in common. Tenants in common share property ownership and any income from such property, but have no *right of survivorship* (see definition). Depending on the state, *real property* (see definition) and/or *personal property* (see definition) may be owned as tenancy in common.

Testator: Refers to the person who made a will, whether or not he or she is alive or dead.

Will: The legal document in which a person can specify who gets what from his or her *estate* (see definition). If a person leaves behind a document that does not comply with his or her state's legal requirements, then it is not a valid will, and legally that person is considered *intestate* (see definition).

Sources of Further Information

Dacey, Norman F. *How to Avoid Probate.* New York: Harper Reference, 1992.

Esperti, Robert A. *Protect Your Estate: A Personal Guide to Intelligent Estate Planning.* New York: McGraw-Hill, 1992.

Kaye, Barry. *Save a Fortune on Your Estate Taxes: Wealth Creation and Preservation.* Homewood, IL.: Business One Irwin, 1992.

Randolph, Mary. *Nolo's Living Trust.* Berkeley, Calif.: Nolo Press, 1991.

Schain, George M. *Estate, Gift, Trust, and Fiduciary Tax Returns: Planning and Preparation.* Colorado Springs, Colo.: Shepard's/McGraw-Hill, 1991.

Shrader, Susan J. G., editor. *Introduction to Estates and Trusts.* St. Paul: West Pub. Co., 1992.

The Editors. *All-States Wills and Estate Planning Guide: Basic Principles and a Summary of State and Territorial Will and Intestacy Statutes.* Chicago: American Bar Association Section of General Practice, 1990.

Weisz, Frank B. *Superkit: The Joint & Last Survivor Strategic Guidebook.* Philadelphia: Wisetone Financial Publications, 1990.

Index

-K-

-L-

-M-

-N-

-O-

–W–

About the Author

Stephen G. Christianson, Esq. practices in Washington, D.C. He is the author of a wide variety of books and legal encyclopedia articles on estate, probate, business law, and other matters. Mr. Christianson has also written *Facts About the Congress* and *The American Book of Days (4th edition)*.